Sign My Name to Freedom

Sign My Name to Freedom

A MEMOIR OF A PIONEERING LIFE

BETTY REID SOSKIN

EDITED BY J. DOUGLAS ALLEN-TAYLOR

HAY HOUSE, INC.
Carlsbad, California • New York City
London • Sydney • Johannesburg
Vancouver • New Delhi

Copyright © 2018 by Betty Reid Soskin

Published and distributed in the United States by: Hay House, Inc.: www
.hayhouse.com® • *Published and distributed in Australia by:* Hay House
Australia Pty. Ltd.: www.hayhouse.com.au • *Published and distributed in the
United Kingdom by:* Hay House UK, Ltd.: www.hayhouse.co.uk • *Distributed in
Canada by:* Raincoast Books: www.raincoast.com • *Published in India by:* Hay
House Publishers India: www.hayhouse.co.in

Cover design: thebookdesigners.com
Interior design: Bryn Starr Best
Indexer: Laura Ogar

Library of Congress Cataloging-in-Publication Data

Names: Soskin, Betty Reid, 1921- author. | Allen-Taylor, J. Douglas, editor.
Title: Sign my name to freedom : a memoir of a pioneering life / Betty Reid
    Soskin ; edited by J. Douglas Allen-Taylor.
Other titles: Memoir of a pioneering life
Description: Carlsbad, California : Hay House, Inc., [2018] | Includes index.
Identifiers: LCCN 2017040961 | ISBN 9781401954215 (hardcover : alk. paper)
Subjects: LCSH: Soskin, Betty Reid, 1921- | African American
    women--California--East Bay--Biography. | Women political
    activists--California--East Bay--Biography. | East Bay (Calif.)--Politics
    and government--20th century. | African Americans--California--East
    Bay--Social conditions--20th century. | College teachers'
    spouses--California--Berkeley--Biography. | Rosie the Riveter/World War II
    Home Front National Historical Park (Agency : U.S.)--Officials and
    employees--Biography. | Creoles--United States--Biography. | San Francisco
    Bay Area--Social life and customs--20th century. | East Bay
    (Calif.)--Biography.
Classification: LCC F868.S156 S67 2018 | DDC 979.4/6053092 [B] --dc23 LC record
available at https://lccn.loc.gov/2017040961

Hardcover ISBN: 978-1-4019-5421-5

10 9 8 7 6 5 4 3 2 1
1st edition, February 2018

Printed in the United States of America

SUSTAINABLE FORESTRY INITIATIVE — Certified Sourcing — www.sfiprogram.org — SFI-01268

SFI label applies to text stock only

IN ANY BOOK ABOUT a life that is reaching toward its 10th decade, far more is going to be left out than can possibly be put in. One regret I have is that there was not room enough to put in more about my four wonderful children.

Because my eldest, Rick, passed away at such an early age, his life is covered in this book from childhood to the short span of his adulthood. But for Bob, David, and Dorian, only their childhood years appear.

David has been dutiful, responsible, and filled with purpose throughout his life. Bob is more of a poet, and much more like me, while David is his father personified. As for Dorian, since she was very young, I've been deeply aware of my responsibility to prepare her throughout life for living without me in it. Although she is confident and reasonably talented, the world is simply not designed for her.

Sign My Name to Freedom is dedicated to the four of them— Rick, Bob, David, and Dorian—the loves and the pride of my life, with the promise that I will take the time to say more about all of them when I write my next book.

CONTENTS

Editor's Note   ix

Prologue   xiii

Chapter 1:   Creole/Black Cajun New Orleans   1

Chapter 2:   Growing Up in Pre-War Bay Area   17

Chapter 3:   Marriage and the War Years   37

Chapter 4:   Into the Lion's Den   55

Chapter 5:   Breaking Down, Breaking Up   75

Chapter 6:   The Movement Years   91

Chapter 7:   An Emancipated Woman   105

Chapter 8:   Richmond and Rosie and Betty the Ranger   131

Chapter 9:   Shining Bright at Twilight:
             Lessons of a Life Long Lived   161

Epilogue   185

Index   191

Acknowledgments   199

About the Author   201

About the Editor   203

Credits   205

EDITOR'S NOTE

WHAT IS THE SECRET OF Betty Reid Soskin's great appeal to so many people both in the country of her birth and around the world? It's a question she and I have been talking over for many years, long before the idea was formed to collect her many writings into a single book about her life.

I have known Betty for, literally, my entire life. She is one of my father's cousins who married into my mother's family, so our lives are intertwined on two sides of our families. It was my delight and privilege to witness her rise to national and international fame and prominence over the last decade or so, and to hold many conversations with her discussing how and why this came to be.

One thing that should be known about Betty is that she never aspired to fame, and has never seen the fame she has attained as the culmination of her life's work. She is constantly both amazed and bewildered by the attention that is paid to her, and, certainly in the beginning days of that fame, dearly worried that she could never live up to the expectations people appeared to lay upon her. I can remember several late-night telephone calls with her in those days when, almost in tears, she wondered what she could possibly say in a speech to be given to some organization or other the next morning. And then the morning would come, and she would stand before those upturned, expectant faces and just be Betty, and she gradually realized that this was exactly what they had come for. I am not at all certain that even to this day she is fully convinced that what she has had to offer is enough.

Because the world did not come to know and appreciate Betty until she was in her 90s, there is a temptation to use her age—and her remarkable retention of a youthful and active mind so late in life—as the main source of her celebrity, but that's only a small part of it.

The elders of our communities are our historians. A historian leads you to the window of the past, presses your nose against the pane, and allows you to see everything that passes by the frame. A good historian walks out the door into the past, walks around, and returns to tell you all he or she has seen so you can understand what the past was like. A great historian—and Betty Reid Soskin is indeed a great historian—takes you by the hand and walks you through the door of the past and allows you to walk around back there, often as far as your own mind can wander, so you can understand what it would have been like to live in those years. She puts you in the past and helps you relive it on your own.

That is one reason this small, slight, unpretentious woman with a voice that rarely rises above a tone of quiet explanation has been able to captivate thousands in talks and lectures around the country.

But another pillar of Betty Reid Soskin's appeal is her unrelenting courage in facing every challenge life places in front of her, whether it is coping with a lifetime of American anti-black racism, raising one developmentally disabled and one gay child, enduring a divorce and a mental breakdown, or beating off a home burglar at the age of 94.

It is that stubborn courage that Betty possesses that is captured in the title of this book, *Sign My Name to Freedom*. The words are the title of a song that Betty, typically, wrote not about herself, but about a woman who had signed up during the civil rights era for the freedom struggle in the Deep South.

There are two ways that we can sign our names to such a freedom struggle: deliberately or by circumstance. Neither should be considered more courageous than the other. Each requires a different type of courage.

The great myth is that the great Rosa Parks took the second way, becoming the symbol of the fight against Jim Crow segregation when she "got tired" one morning and refused to give up her seat on a Montgomery, Alabama, bus to a white passenger. It did not happen that way. Ms. Rosa was the secretary of the Montgomery NAACP, and she trained for many months at the Highlander Research and Education Center in Tennessee to prepare for the well-planned action. When she got on the bus that morning she intended to keep her seat, knowing that she would almost certainly be jailed, and possibly suffer even worse. Her actions resulted from a conscious choice to step to the front rank of the fight for freedom.

It was Betty Reid Soskin who took the path we mistakenly assign to Rosa Parks. Betty rarely chose her life's battles in advance, as Rosa did. Instead, she faced them as they came—working, raising a family, choosing a home, operating a business on her own. Her sign-ups for the freedom fight were generally unplanned and spontaneous, and in that, she showed all of us what ordinary citizens facing up to their fears can accomplish.

This book was first conceived by Tavis Smiley and Hay House as Betty Reid Soskin's life story in her own words. They had read portions of her blog, *CBreaux Speaks*, which is faithfully and lovingly followed by thousands around the world, and saw Betty's enormous talent at recounting incidents in her life in powerful, emotional writing. But turning those blog writings into a full autobiography presented a challenge because, just as she used to do with her song composing, Betty writes entirely in the moment. Her writings of past events are caused by emotional triggers: a rediscovered old photograph, an anniversary, a memory suddenly recalled. Her writing process can be described by Omar Khayyám's dictum that "the moving finger writes and, having writ, moves on." A change made in her writing style to accommodate a full autobiography would rob her writing of all its life and all we have come to value it for.

And so, a compromise was reached.

The early portions of Betty's life, much of which she has not dealt with in her blog, are covered by taking her words from two long interviews she did with the Regional Oral History Office (now the Oral History Center) of the Bancroft Library of the University of California at Berkeley. The remainder of the book consists of excerpts from Betty's blog. Both the interview excerpts and the blog entries have been rearranged in chronological or, at times, subject-matter order. Therefore, there are gaps in the narrative of her life. We have tried to bridge those gaps, where appropriate, with editor's notes. The result, we feel, is a beautiful book that fulfills the original promise of telling the story of Betty Reid Soskin's life in Betty's own words.

It is my sincere hope that you take as much pleasure in reading it as I derived from whatever small hand I had in bringing it to life.

J. Douglas Allen-Taylor
Oakland, California
July 2017

PROLOGUE

THEY ARE MAKING A film about me. Two films, in fact.

One of the fine filmmakers appeared with his team to conduct an on-camera interview to feed into the 30-minute work that is now nearing completion after more than three years of shooting. I'm learning a lot about filmmaking in the process, and the producer, Carl Bidleman, tells me that they now have produced about 50 hours of work that—after editing—will become that 30-minute film for the National Park Service. The end may be in sight.

The release date has not yet been set as I write this, but I suspect that it might be late fall 2017 or early winter.

I imagine that the editing may be the most satisfying part of the process, but I'm projecting here, and have no real sense of what really goes into filmmaking. It was fascinating to see them—after the actual interview was over, and just before the complicated setup of lights and cameras was being disassembled—they called for a "hush" while the room's ambiance was recorded through the cameras. When questioned, Carl explained that this was needed for the editing, for blending fragments of scenes together without blank silences.

After this extended period of being filmed, it doesn't take more than a few minutes to forget the process, the cameras, and hear just the questions, and to react without self-consciousness. I'd never have guessed this would ever be possible, but it most assuredly happens with experience over time, once those behind the cameras have become simply trusted and good friends, eventually, of long standing.

What the end result will be I cannot imagine. But maybe this works for me since I rarely spend much time in yesterday or tomorrow (except when it's called for in my work). There has always simply been *"Now!"* I suspect that this attitude is a holdover from childhood, just something that I've never outgrown.

I've lived my entire life in a constant state of surprise, rarely borrowing from the future or regretting the past, which tends to keep the present always alive and guess-worthy. Anticipation could not have improved this ongoing new reality that sets me right in the middle of the Art of Others, something that has become increasingly exciting as I've grown older. I feel like an ever-evolving collaborator in training.

The filmmaking has become organic, much as my work with the National Park Service has become over time. There, I'm but one element in the visitor experience, which includes orientation films, life-cast figures, documentation of the World War II Home Front story, all the works of other rangers, historians, writers, artists, fabricators, lighting designers, etc., and me!

It is also true of the book that is set for release in February 2018, which is being edited by Jesse Douglas Allen-Taylor from a combination of my oral histories (archived at the Bancroft Library at UC Berkeley) and this blog. It is to be published by Hay House out of New York, and it will bring together their writers and editors with my collected words. These often unrelated essays on cabbages and kings, (at times) pure rants, and, sometimes, prayers will become an amalgamation of all those talents and minds, and I will again be a part of something larger than myself.[1]

A thought that has never occurred to me before this very moment: what greater exit from this dimension than to simply disappear into the works of others? That might be the *perfect* way to move gracefully into whatever immortality there is, just to blend seamlessly into the whole with little notice. Maybe this insight has moved out from the subconscious to provide a rationale for whatever comes next . . . whenever . . .

---

1 *EDITOR'S NOTE:* The book Betty is referring to is, of course, this one.

Who on earth would ever have imagined that my little living room would become a movie set on occasion, and that I would become at 95 a "star" sitting at my dining room table, comfortable in my socks and non-glamorous cotton trousers, and as relaxed as a cat on a windowsill basking in the noonday sun!

Yet that is precisely where we are in life on this day, June 9, 2017.

THIS TIME I'M ADDING to the voice-over thread to be filled in behind related images of the other documentary (90-minute) by Bryan Gibel, the filmmaker/producer of the other film being made about me.

For the second day in a row (unusual), I found myself seated in a quickly created "bunker" of quilted blankets hooked together to make a kind of sound booth and going over old history—not the kind that deals with the WWII Home Front, but "Betty" history, which turns out to be far deeper and with an emotional content that is only hinted at in the national stories, or of a different kind, at least.

In the aftermath, I've found myself today going back over that interview and finding places where there are glaring contradictions and inconsistencies:

Where much of the interview was taken up with how thoroughly I'd discounted the artist part of myself in running away from my brief encounter with the entertainment industry, nonetheless I've certainly written about that side of myself in this journal, and rather unsparingly. In fact, *she* holds a prominent place in my personal narrative, even while I'm denying her existence.

I wonder if the fact that over time, she has evolved as a third person, somehow severed her from the whole, a "she." Though there is clearly some recent movement occurring, at integrating into a more complex Betty, at a time when I'm being forced under the scrutiny of filmmaking to incorporate all of me into coherence. But is that consistent with real life? Am I not, alternately, *all* of those splintered pieces, and does the weaving together of all of those divergent bits and pieces not present the next challenge in this final decade?

Maybe that younger creative artist Betty was never "disappeared" at all, but has been dormant, waiting patiently in the wings to reappear at some auspicious time when the barriers were lowered and this final integration was possible. At a time when there was no marriage to save nor children to raise, no aging parents to caretake, no business to reclaim as a legacy for our kids, no handicapped daughter to prepare for my exit, just maybe . . .

It's beginning to feel that way as I sit behind the west gallery exhibit at the bayside windows of the Visitor Education Center at the Rosie the Riveter/World War II Homefront National Historical Park, waiting to present my two o'clock program. That perch allows me to become disconnected from those gathering at the front desk for their tickets long enough to find the quiet offered by idly watching the bands of fog silently drift in over the water, the changing light, the wind playing capriciously in the branches of that giant eucalyptus tree, the rising and lowering of the tides, that ever-changing vista of Brooks Island, the East Bay hills, the San Francisco skyline, the moody panoramic bay view, shorebirds in constant flight, windsurfers skating over the waters precariously, the occasional leisurely passage of a sailboat . . .

Often of late, I draw my cell phone out of the pocket of my uniform, press the button for music, and, holding it to my ear so that voice won't bleed out into the gallery, listen secretly to my younger self of 40 years ago singing the life I was living when my songs were birthed, and that life returns with all of the affect it carried at the time. There are times when it takes more than a moment to bring myself back into the present.

But then it's time to creep down the back stairs to enter our little theater where I, alone, sit on that kitchen stool and watch as those inquiring strangers begin to enter *my* space in twos and threes until the room is full, and the stories begin and a quite *different* past comes alive again, once more, and we're sharing that *other* journey back through time . . .

And as complicated as it sounds, it is *I* who serve as the connecting link to what are on the surface conflicting realities, but equally authentic and equally true.

What happens to "I rarely spend time regretting the past or anticipating the future; there is only NOW"? That's a fine example of *conflicting truths*, a concept that arrived unannounced shortly after my 90th birthday, an axiom that I stubbornly believe to be not only possible but an important fact of life.

Yet, it *is* all of a piece, is it not?

It is in these moments that I am beginning to feel all the parts of myself coming together, and the distance between them lessening, and the hope that, in time, over continuing days, weeks, and months under the scrutiny necessary for meaningful filmmaking, I will become whole, perhaps for the very first time, like metal shavings attracted irresistibly to a magnet.

I'm fairly certain that meanwhile, I'm in for some highly emotional moments as that integration process takes over.

The prize is that somehow I've developed the ability to place myself out of range and watch that process as it unfolds. I suspect that it is this ability that allows me to learn from it all, and to use it in my work. *I'm able to become a spectator to myself.* To see myself *in context.*

There is the sense that, in these final years, I'm being all of the women that I've become over time, and using everything that I've ever experienced in reaching this remarkable time of life. It's all incorporated into that aging woman sitting on that kitchen stool before those audiences of 48 friendly strangers every Tuesday, Thursday, and Saturday on into infinity.

I suspect that it may be time to pull those curtains back and let the sun in, to let the music play, as I live all of the complex layers of my existence simultaneously . . .

1

CREOLE/BLACK CAJUN NEW ORLEANS

I WAS BORN ON September 22, 1921, in Detroit, Michigan, where my parents settled after leaving New Orleans for the first time. Dad was a millwright/engineer. My sister Marjorie had been born there in 1918. In 1924, my paternal grandfather died in New Orleans, and the family returned to live with my father's mother, on Lapeyrouse Street. I was only three when we moved back to New Orleans, so I've never really known anything about Michigan.

I have memories of New Orleans before we left for California. I can remember when I was three and four years old, and that was before I even began to consciously seek out history.

I have images in my head of the first time I was allowed to walk to the store alone. I have images in my head of standing on top of a huge wooden chest outside of the grocery store, in which ice and oysters were kept. And the men in the community would be out cracking oysters and drinking beer, and I remember my dad standing me atop this wooden chest and my singing, "In a Little Spanish Town." I must have been four. But I have images of the time being separated out and sitting on the front lawn when my baby sister was born. I remember the house, I remember falling and bumping my head after sitting on some sort of reel the hose was kept on. I have memories of a great flood that hit and sleeping on mattresses atop wooden crates to be above the water that was in the house. I remember a lot of things about being a small child in Louisiana.

I remember my father telling me that when my grandfather died, because he was such a great man in the Creole part of New Orleans—downtown—because he was such a special man, his body lay in state on the altar for three days so that the community could pay homage. So he was a big man, and I knew that. My dad's pride in his father was unbounded.

I remember my grandmother, my father's mother. Her name was Victoria Morales Charbonnet. We called her Ma-mair.

I remember once I was sitting on the front porch on Lapeyrouse Street at a duplex that my grandparents lived in. I remember sitting in Ma-mair's lap, and you know how women have this fleshy part of their arms between the elbow and the shoulder? I remember cuddling that, holding it.

I can remember brushing her hair for long, long periods, her waist-length hair. Her hair was heavy, very dark, coarse, and straight. Her parents were Isleños from the Canary Islands, heavily Spanish, named Morales. What I remember of her is that kind of image. She was blind, from diabetes. And I guess the way a blind person takes care of a child is they keep them close, they hold them as much as possible. I can almost smell my grandmother, I have a deep sense of her, though I can't visualize her, I don't remember what she looked like, and there are no surviving pictures of her. But I remember holding on to her lower arm, or her upper arm underneath, and brushing her hair. I learned how to braid on my grandmother's hair, and I must have been four.

My grandmother was my caretaker and best friend. She took care of me by having me brush her long hair and telling me stories without end. Most of her stories were told in a language I didn't understand, but when you're that age, who cares? It's the feelings that count, and her message was always one of love. She died shortly after we moved to California.

My younger sister, Lottie, was born when I was four years old. We were living on Frenchmen Street in a two-story house. On that day, my uncle Dr. Raleigh Coker (the husband of my mother's great-aunt Emily) was the attending physician, and various aunts were running around doing whatever it is that aunts do at such times. Me? I was out in the front yard, sitting on one of those metal gizmos a garden hose is wound around. It began to roll. I fell backward and cracked my head on the sidewalk! The raised scar is still there, marking the day of my little sister's birth!

Shortly thereafter, in big-sister style, I remember being allowed for the first time to walk all the way to Aunt Corinne's house on Touro Street (maybe two blocks), which was unpaved, with boardwalks. Boards were put down by the city in summer to walk on and lifted in winter by residents of the community to burn in their stoves for heat. I believe that would have been in the Seventh Ward.

I have other flashes of memory of my brief childhood in New Orleans. Sitting on front porches on hot and humid summer evenings while the neighbors cruised by, men tipping their hats and doing their "Good evenin's" and women flirting, I suppose. Sweet lost bread and jambalaya. Red beans and rice. Cream cheese that in no way resembles what goes by that name today, but a confection that came in a small round carton and had a sweet cream sauce over it. Soft-shelled crabs and crawfish feeds with newspaper tablecloths. Seafood gumbo. Red "jumbo" soda water bought in pitchers brought from home. *Lagniappe!*—the catchphrase that always ended the trip to the corner store and guaranteed a piece of candy, a few crackers, peanuts, anything extra. Californians, sadly, knew nothing about lagniappe.

I remember disturbing pictures of Jesus everywhere, crucifixes on walls, an altar to the Virgin Mary. There was the musty smell while sleeping under mosquito netting, the chamber pot under the bed for nighttime use, the blue-and-white ceramic pitcher and bowl on the nightstand beside the bed. There was the scurrying of roaches when lamps were lit at night. The kerosene stove in the middle of the living room and lacy antimacassars on every piece of parlor furniture. There was the huge armoire in Ma-mair's bedroom that held heaven knows what, and the cedar chest at the foot of her bed that smelled of camphor when she drew extra blankets from it. There were candles, oil lamps in case of power failures, and incense in those tiny little pyramid shapes. I remember someone's Spanish shawl that was artfully draped over a chair, and that must have had some history.

THERE WERE WONDERFUL STORIES that my dad used to tell me about New Orleans. They were always family stories. Dad's was a huge, devout Catholic family. Over her lifetime, his mother had given birth to 17 children, though only seven boys and our girls survived childhood. But the stories were always about his brothers, always crazy stories about them, and many of them I suspected were lies told purely to entertain. My mother would be standing behind my father and laughing—"Don't you listen to him!" And he would tell these wild stories about his brothers. He would tell these wild stories about these brothers that were just wonderfully crazy, and I wish I could remember them now, but I can only remember sitting listening to them, spellbound.

My mother's side of the family also had stories about being Creole. Mother had some really wild, crazy Creole characters in her family.

There was a cousin Olga, my mother's first cousin, who was a character, this huge woman. I met her when I was 15 and my parents sent me down to New Orleans on a trip to be that year's delegate to represent our branch of the family at the annual birthday celebration for my great-grandmother, Mammá. You'd go into Olga's typical 19th-century-style New Orleans house and there was a jukebox in the living room. Then I learned later that this was the place in New Orleans where all the big bands who came through—the ones that couldn't stay at hotels because blacks couldn't stay there—they stayed at Big Olga's. Hers was the place where everybody went. So if you wanted to see any of the sidemen, Duke Ellington, Louis Jordan, Jimmie Lunceford, all these people, they all stayed at Big Olga's. I think that in today's economy, Olga would be described as being in the hospitality industry.

Well, eventually, Big Olga—Mother used to tell this story and just laugh—opened a bar near her home, and she named it the Holy Bar. The reason was that the priest in the parish had given her some of the old altar cloths from Corpus Christi Catholic Church that could no longer be mended. She placed the altar cloths on the bar where the drinks were served, to the dismay of poor Father Kelly! I mean, Olga was as sacrilegious as anybody could be.

This was during the years of formal segregation, and at that time, when black people got on the streetcar in New Orleans, you had to sit in the back. There was this thing—what they called the bar—that you could slip into the slots at the back of the seats to mark the white section from the black section. White people could move it back to make more room for white people, but black people couldn't move it up. Olga got on a streetcar one time and there were no seats left in the back, so she picked the bar up and moved it up to make room for herself. And the conductor—who knew her well because this was the line she always rode on—came back and told her she couldn't do that. And she said yes she could and he wasn't going to stop her. They took her downtown and off to jail off the streetcar because, simply, she was going to beat them all up with the bar.

MY PARENTS' SOCIAL LIFE in New Orleans revolved around being Creole. That was status. Those Creoles were also barbers; they were dentists; they were redcaps; they were postal workers. They were teachers, pharmacists, doctors, dentists, tradesmen, craftsmen, and occupied all of the social roles needed in a community where professional services were denied due to racism. Throughout the South at the time, there was a strong professional class by necessity. Women didn't have the status men did. But their status wasn't based upon money. It was based upon names. And the Charbonnets of New Orleans were a very, very old family.

According to recent research, the parents of my paternal grandmother, Victoria, the Moraleses, came from St. Bernard Parish in Louisiana. They were what was called Isleños, and St. Bernard Parish was where most of these former Spanish settlers lived. As the French who settled in the New World came to be known as the Creoles, so the Spanish became the Isleños. They had settled there when the Spanish were dominating New Orleans. My father's family arrived in New Orleans from Thiers, France, before the Louisiana Purchase. They were two brothers who I've come to believe were escaping the French Revolution. One of them went to Haiti. He died there, but his family later made it back to the United States. We were on the wrong side of the Haitian Revolution, apparently. Not the rebel leader Toussaint L'Ouverture's side.

Our family homes were in the Tremé in New Orleans, the section bordered by the French Quarter. The Tremé was downtown, and was the site of Corpus Christi Catholic Church, which my grandfather, Louis Charbonnet, built. It was the Creole section. Creoles lived downtown, Americans lived uptown, and Canal Street divided them.

My dad described people other than Creoles as Americans. It wasn't just my father. I used to kind of laugh at that. My sense of it is that the Creoles were the people who were related by blood to both sides, racially. They were usually better educated, and were treated quite differently.[2]

My father and grandfather built the first convent for black nuns, for the Sisters of the Holy Family, which was the first black order of nuns in this country. My dad's younger brother, Louis, was a contractor. Like his father and brothers, he also was a builder. Most of the seven boys were builders of one kind or another.

Louis and another contractor, who was a white Charbonnet named Paul, used Canal Street as the dividing line, so that all the jobs that came up on the white side would go to Paul Charbonnet, and all the jobs that came up on the Creole side would go to my Uncle Louis. There was this understanding between the white and black Charbonnets, and these two contractors worked with that to the benefit of both families.

My father used to tell the story that if any of his seven brothers got into trouble and were taken downtown to the courthouse, Judge Charbonnet—who was white—would take him into the back room, talk to him, pat him on the fanny, and send him back home. Tell him that he was from a special class of people. They were not treated in the same way as ordinary African Americans.

---

2   EDITOR'S NOTE: In other words, Betty's father called all non-Creoles "Americans," regardless of whether they were white or African American. Creoles related to both white folks and African Americans, and they were treated differently by whites than African Americans were treated.

I later rebelled against that when I was growing up, because it seemed like another form of racism to me.

BEING A CREOLE, HOWEVER, was only a thin layer of protection against the great weight of racism that was prevalent in the South of those days. And that protection could easily be rolled away.

When I was growing up, I learned from my parents that they originally relocated from New Orleans to Detroit before they had children so that my father could get work in one of the auto plants up there. It was not until I returned to New Orleans in 2012 that I learned the true reason from my cousin, Armand, whose father had been my own father's brother.

"It was awful!" Armand told me.

He said that my father and my grandfather, Louis Charbonnet, were working on a job together when a white man came up to ask my grandfather a question.

"As you know," Armand said, "in those times, no white man ever addressed a black person by their last name."

And that's what this white man did, calling my proud grandfather "Louis," using the regular French pronunciation of "Louie." On that note, my equally proud father called the white man on it, saying, "Do you know who you're talking to?" And he followed that impertinent question by doing something that was equally forbidden for a black man in the South at the time, calling the white man by his own first name.

"Grandfather had to rush him out of the state and to Detroit where your mother had relatives until it was safe to come home," cousin Armand told me.

That must have been in about 1917 and my mother was probably pregnant with my sister, Marjorie. We returned to New Orleans shortly after I was born four years later, when my grandfather's health failed.

GROWING UP IN NEW ORLEANS, I didn't know there was anything such as a white Creole. Creoles were always people who were mixed. They were French, Spanish, Native American, and African. And they were a class of people who were simply separated out. They had their own proud culture.

Skin color among the Creoles of New Orleans was no big thing since Creoles come in all colors and types and were the offspring of blacks and whites and lived in a kind of racial limbo, somewhere in between, both socially and racially. We were the romantic quadroons and octoroons of the times, and in many instances, the paramours of the upper-class white population, though that's surely less true in more recent times.

I do know that there was a regular crossing of the color line for better-paying jobs. There was always some regret, but also a tacit agreement that no one would inform on family members who took that route. I'm still aware of cousins who married and disappeared into the greater population without a trace.

Some years ago my father's youngest brother, Melbourne, came to spend a few days with us. While he was here a dear friend of my husband, Bill, Dr. Leonard Duhl, and his wife came over to dinner. Leonard presented me with a program from a performance of *Madame Butterfly* that he'd attended at the San Francisco Opera. Leonard noted that in the cast of *Madame Butterfly* was Patricia Charbonnet, who played the lead. Leonard knew that this was my maiden name. I said to Leonard, "But she's surely not related to us. She's obviously a member of the white branch of the family." Uncle Mel snorted but held his peace until the Duhls had gone. Then he followed me out to the kitchen as I cleared the table and said, "I wanna tell you something, hon. Huey Long had a sayin' that you could feed all the *really* white folks in Louisiana offa one chicken!"

In other words, a lot of folks in Louisiana who were claiming to be white were not always fully so.

I also remember the story of a clerk who toiled in the basement of the courthouse in New Orleans selling birth certificates with the race designated as white to light-skinned black people, at a lower price for children, a higher price for adults.

But many of the New Orleans Creoles were content with the fact that they had their own well-developed culture with its traditions proudly drawn from many parts of the world.

I don't recall ever hearing my maternal grandmother, Mammá, speak anything but Creole, a patois of French. Aunt Vivian, Aunt Annabelle, and my mother—all those in that generation and all those raised in St. James Parish in Mammá's household—were bilingual. They spoke in English but gossiped in Creole, which was the main language of their household. My generation only spoke English, though you could hear a few expressions in Creole from my Aunt Belle's daughters, who were of my generation and were raised in California. But few others of the California clan retained those rich bilingual speech patterns.

In my parents' household and the household of many of the older family members who migrated to California, it was common for adults to start out in one language and drift in and out of the other without warning. The kids were never included, since Creole was reserved as the means for transmitting gossip, grown-up to grown-up, as with most immigrant families.

I regret now that they didn't pay more attention, because I think there was more to be salvaged there than even I was aware of. But speaking French didn't matter in California, and they didn't teach it to their children. And now that I'm in my early 80s and looking back on a culture that's disappearing, I regret it. I wish I had listened harder to the stories. I wish I had paid more attention.

MY MOTHER WAS Lottie Allen, Lottie Estelle Allen. She was from the Breaux family. She was from a Creole-Cajun line of people in St. James Parish, Louisiana.

My mother was the Creole-Cajun black, my father was the Creole black. My father came from what he saw as aristocracy, and my mother came from the country, St. James. Early on, I got the sense of the difference.

The Cajun line of people are the people who—at least according to the part of the family history I've done—arrived from

Loudun, France, back in 1631, the first of the Breaux family. That coincides with the witch-burning period, though I don't know how those things connect. They left France; they arrived in Nova Scotia, where they settled for a number of years—generations. They then migrated from Nova Scotia into Maryland, and from Maryland they received a land grant from the Spanish who had then settled in Louisiana Territory and wound up in St. James Parish, Louisiana, which became the—they were the Acadians, who were the French who became the Cajuns. My mother, I can only go back to her grandmother Leontine (Mammá) because the slave curtain drops and you can't get anywhere before about 1830. But that is her side of the family.

Leontine's mother was Celestine "of no last name," a house servant at the plantation of Edouard Breaux, a Cajun landowner, whom she later married. Among my papers is the marriage certificate retrieved from the Catholic Diocese in Baton Rouge. It is written in French, bearing his signature and her *X*. The date of the marriage was October 1865, only a few months after the fall of the Confederacy and the end of slavery in America. Leontine was 19 at the time of her parents' marriage. And, yes, Edouard Breaux was the master who owned them both.

Freedom came for both Leontine and her mother, but not before the day of the proclamation.

I remember clearly the day cousin Ruth (the daughter of Isabel Allen LeBeouf Warnie, the granddaughter of Leontine and the great-granddaughter of Celestine) and I were driving back from the Golden Gate National Cemetery in San Bruno after discovering the earliest microfiche records of our great-grandmother. Then there was the day that the marriage records turned up in the archives of the Catholic Diocese of Baton Rouge in the form of a brief statement written in French attesting to the marriage between Edouard and Celestine.

In going back through a voluminous packet of legal documents received from the National Archives some years ago, along with those family stories I learned as an inquisitive teenager, I've been able to pull together a picture of those lives. You can imagine my surprise and delight to discover this important marriage document that proved that the family lore that told of how the Cajun people—who were agrarians—worked the fields with their slaves, and that it was fairly common for deep friendships to be formed, and marriages between Cajuns and black folks were often seen. Apparently Edouard and Celestine had been in a common-law relationship throughout Leontine's 19 years and married in a Catholic ceremony as soon as it was possible to do so after the signing of the Emancipation Proclamation.

I'd assumed that after she married Edouard, my great-great grandmother on my mother's side, Celestine, had an intact family that consisted of herself, her husband, Edouard, her daughter, Leontine, who was my great-grandmother, and a son named Theophile, whom we've lost track of. According to diocesan records, three-year-old Theophile's birth was legitimized by the marriage. I remember wondering, just how had it been possible to limit that little family to two children, and by what method was their spacing accomplished?

But the important fact to me was that, atypically of many black family histories that included a mixing of slave masters and the enslaved, ours had not resulted from rape or sexual exploitation, but rather there was a traceable familial relationship sanctioned by the church. How naïve was I?

I suppose I was so wedded to that positive story that when we later received documents from the War Department that included testimonies by neighbors and friends in St. James in support of a widow's pension for Leontine, I failed to notice that Leontine had provided the name of her father as *Sylvestre* Breaux, who is listed in the census of the time as Edouard's older brother.

A cousin recently suggested that perhaps Celestine had been raped 19 years earlier than the 1865 date of her mother's marriage to Edouard, and that Leontine had been aware of her actual parentage all of her life.

I suspect that rape would have been so common at that time that it would have been of no particular importance in the scheme of things. In 1846, more than a dozen years after the British outlawed slavery in 1833, American slave owners were producing their own "stock" by forcibly impregnating their female slaves. They were doing so in order to compete in the marketplace, in order to have chattel to pass along to their heirs, and in order to preserve the Southern economy and the time-honored Southern way of life, which had been built upon the slave trade. I've never gotten over the fact that those planters were quite literally *producing and selling their own children*. Under those circumstances, it was necessary that blacks be regarded as less than human. Were that not so, the entire system would have been undermined. You can imagine that such a practice would have been one of the inhumane results of human bondage that ended with the Emancipation Proclamation but was left out of history books in defense of our national integrity, or at least the integrity that we claim in theory.

But then, I would not have been viewed as part of the "we" at that time, since white male supremacy ruled the day, much as it has since that time. White supremacy along with white privilege have been prohibitive of social change and have resisted any attempt at altering the lens through which we see "American" life in the century that followed.

Small wonder that we've never been able to process that history. It says horrific things about us as a nation and our trail of cruelty and abusiveness since African Americans landed on these shores.

MY MOTHER'S FATHER was the eldest in a family of 14 or 15 children. His mother, Mammá—Leontine Breaux Allen—was widowed late in the 19th century, left with many of the younger children still in the household. Her husband, George, had served in the Civil War for the North, a member of the 1st Louisiana Native Guard.

The lovely family tale is that Leontine was sitting in her front yard pecan tree when the soldiers came marching down the road. George Allen broke ranks and coaxed her down from the limb and carried her on his shoulders for more than a mile before letting her down. He later became a boarder in the New Orleans home of a family member and their courtship continued. I once believed my great-grandfather George was from Ohio, though I am not certain now where I got that impression, and documents I later received relating to his Army pension benefits indicated that he may have grown up in New Orleans among other members of that branch of the Allen family. George remains a shadowy figure in our lives, without even a photograph to remind us of his existence. It's said that there once was a large portrait of him hanging on the wall of their little home beside the levee in St. James Parish, but that home was destroyed by fire long after Leontine's death, and the photo must have been devoured by the flames.

George and Mammá's eldest son, also named George, married my mother's mother, Julia, known as Minette, who was 14 at the time. They had one child, who was my mother. And when my mother was seven months old, Minette died, so my grandfather brought my mother back to Mammá's house to be raised.

This was a little house that Mammá owned that was on a strip back from the Mississippi River in Welcome, St. James Parish, Louisiana. The house is no longer there. My mother grew up there. Her father, whom we called Papa George, went out and remarried a second woman of Spanish descent, Desirée Fernandez. They had five children and when that second wife died, he brought those children back to Mammá as well, and they grew up in Mammá's household along with my mother, who was the eldest grandchild.

My mother grew up in this household of 15 to 20 children. They worked the farm, they took care of things, they took care of each other, they educated each other. Eventually the older children began to leave St. James and move into town, which was New Orleans. But my mother, being the first, didn't get in on that, so she never left the country until she married my father when they were both 19.

I WAS PRIVILEGED TO have actually known my slave ancestor, Leontine Breaux Allen. I first got to meet her during a visit to New Orleans when I was about 16. She was born into slavery in 1846 and died in 1948 at the age of 102. I was a 27-year-old married woman and mother of two when she died, three years after the end of WWII.

My mother, who was born in the year 1894, lived to be 101. Miscegenation clearly does not foul the gene pool.

My mother's younger sister, Aunt Vivian Allen-Jernigan, adored her grandmother. Vivian told stories of the slavery days, of Mammá and Mammá's mother, Celestine, cooking in the kitchen of their plantation owner, Edouard Breaux, and walking down to the fields three times a day, bringing meals to the field hands. Vivian also loved to tell about how years later when she, Vivian, was a small child, once the chores were completed in the fields, and at the end of the day, "Mammá would sink into the living room rocking chair and with an ever-so-slight motion with her hand would send me to a secret place beside the fireplace to bring forth a little corncob pipe and tobacco pouch from behind a loose brick. She made me feel as if this was a secret shared between us," Aunt Vivian would continue. "She would then send me to bed while she remained seated, silently drawing on her pipe until the house of many people would settle down for the night. It was only then that she would climb under the mosquito netting of the big bed until the first morning light."

BY FAR THE MOST INTRIGUING STORY about my mother's grandmother had to do with the critical role she played in her little community in St. James Parish, Louisiana. Mammá was the town "medical assistant," serving as "intern" for Dr. Hydel, the circuit-rider doctor who came through on horseback about every three months to provide what medical services there were for the people of the parish. Mammá also served as the town's midwife and delivered not only the babies of the family's women, but also the babies of most of the women in their village. I suspect that this would have been for African Americans only, though I'm not sure about this.

During the few days before the doctor's visit, it was she who rode her horse through St. James calling on all those who might need medical attention. The routine was that she'd place a white towel on the gatepost of each home where help was needed, and this determined just where the doctor would stop. He would confer with Mammá on patients' aftercare, and she was accountable for their health issues until his return months later.

Those stories made her one of my personal heroes early in life, and during the 1995 honoring ceremonies, when I was named one of 10 outstanding women by the National Women's History Project, I had cause to wonder. One never feels worthy, I suppose, but I came to terms with the proceedings upon realizing that I'd spent my whole life never seeking public office or acclaim (though surely I was courted from time to time), but instead, I'd been completely satisfied to find fulfillment in draping symbolic "white towels" over imaginary gateposts anywhere help might be needed throughout not only my community, but also as a field representative for California's 14th Assembly District in later life, and now in my role with the National Park Service.

It is Mammá's work that provides shape and form to mine to this day, and she is cited in my commentaries at the twice-weekly theater presentations at the Rosie the Riveter national park—and with great pride and humility. She and I are players in the great American narrative, as are so many extraordinary ordinary people.

2

GROWING UP
IN PRE-WAR
BAY AREA

I USED TO BELIEVE that I was four years old when we arrived in California. But since then, I've discovered that the age I actually came at was six. I know that because as I looked back, I could remember New Orleans's Great Flood and the great storms that preceded it, and that took place in 1927, when I was six.

And then I remembered the trauma. I'm phobic about lightning and thunder. I've never understood why. I've never had any reason to understand. But I remember my grandmother telling me to jump into bed at the first sound of thunder because had I ever heard of anyone being struck by lightning in bed? And all the way into my adulthood, I would jump into bed the minute thunder rolled.

So I began to connect that great storm with my entry into California. I remembered that that was a reason we came to California. I began to realize why I would have buried that time, because it was so traumatic. It completely uprooted and changed my life. I was a child in New Orleans, then suddenly I was in my grandfather's home in California. And it also seemed to have been connected to the fact that I was born into a strongly Catholic family.

That storm happened on Good Friday. So the symbolism, the religious symbolism, also would've been traumatic.[3]

The storm lasted for days, it seems, and left me with images of my bed stacked on orange crates with water lapping just below. The house filled with the tide and everything lost. Dad building a square-bottomed boat and ferrying neighbors to and from wherever they needed to go for supplies, with Marjorie and a little boy cousin going along to bail water as they rowed.

Quiet, desperate grown-ups' conversations, and—when the water receded—worms everywhere and the smell I will never forget.

The rice mill that our family owned, where Dad was working, stood idle, its machinery hopelessly rusted when the water went down. Everything was lost. Mother packed all that was left (three little girls and the crucifix, I believe) and headed west to join her father, Papa George. The western branch of the family now had three sons and my mother's younger sister, who had followed Papa George. Aunt Vivian was a student at the University of California at Berkeley. Uncles Fred, Lloyd, and Herman had all found work with the Southern Pacific Railroad, and Papa George was a waiter at the then-exclusive Oakland Athletic Club. Dad would follow after things were settled back home in New Orleans.

I remember the train trip, but mostly because poor little Marjorie had left home wearing a green taffeta dress that was a costume Mother had made for some special occasion. It had disintegrated into green ribbons by the time we reached our destination.

Papa George met us at the 16th Street Railroad Station in Oakland, California, in his new Model T Ford (black, of course) with a rumble seat, and we rode out to East Oakland to our new home on 76th Avenue.

---

3   *EDITOR'S NOTE:* Jesus was crucified on Good Friday, and, according to the biblical accounts, at the time of his crucifixion there occurred several supernatural events, including the darkening of the sky for three hours and earthquakes that caused the bursting open of graves, allowing the holiest of the dead to walk the earth again. Priests' sermons and folktales would have amplified on these phenomena, and many felt that their recurrence would signal the second coming of the Christ and the ending of the world. Many Louisiana Christians thought the floods of 1927 signaled those prophesized events.

It actually turned out not to be ours at all, but his and Aunt Vivian's, and Uncle Lloyd's, and Papa's third wife, Louise's. As I recall, it was really a tiny house set in a huge expanse of meadow and had only three small bedrooms, so I'm not sure how we all managed, but not unlike the way that other immigrants to the Golden State handled that, I suppose.

There was Papa's vegetable garden taking up some of the space, and about a block away, with nothing in between, was very German Mr. Mueller's dairy farm, where he kept a large herd of black-and-white cows that were pastured just outside our house. Papa bartered vegetables for milk with the Muellers. Sometimes I got to help carry the zucchini and corn and string beans and whatever else was ready, and watch Mrs. Mueller at the churn.

To the west there were two railroad tracks, the Southern Pacific and the Western Pacific, separated by wetlands and endless miles of cattails and willows. The swamplands ran uninterrupted for miles, ending at the bay. At the end of the wetlands, across a two-lane highway, were the two hangars of the just-developing Oakland Airport. There was one hangar and a flight school at the time, I believe.

On the land where Papa George's little house stood there is now a huge iron foundry. Across the road there is a network of highways that interface at just that point and then divide and go to the airport, the highly developed Hegenberger Road commercial and office park developments, and the Oakland Coliseum, home of the Oakland Raiders. Not sure just what Mr. Mueller's dairy disappeared under, but there are few signs that it ever existed.

There is an effort now by local environmentalists to reinstate the wetlands in some of that area, and I've had a recent opportunity to stand on the deck of the Martin Luther King Jr. Regional Shoreline Park that overlooks the new nature sanctuary that joins the Oakland estuary, right there on the lands where I caught pollywogs and butterflies lo those many years ago. Where we "smoked" cattails and where salamanders, dragonflies, and all sorts of crawly creatures were collected and brought home in jelly jars to satisfy my curiosity, insatiable even then. Where we so often saw hobos with their worldly possessions tied on a stick carried across their shoulders, following the tracks to wherever they would take them. It was the Depression era, and we didn't look on these men as sinister, only interesting, to be invited home to sit on the back porch to share whatever might be left over from the night before. Mother was never fearful of them, as I recall. We loved the stories from those willing to share. It was a different time, surely.

Were we poor?

Funny, that might be the least relevant term to use when referring to Creole people or culture. That's simply not an accurate measure of worth for us. I'm certain—were I using the values of the European acquisitive and materialistic society that now forms the adopted values of my life—that word might be fitting. But in the context of New Orleans and all that flowed therefrom, economic worth is fairly irrelevant.

I know about Mom getting up early on Thursday mornings to be among the first to "Sally Ann's" (the Salvation Army store) for the best pickin's because that was the day the truck delivered new old stuff to the local store. I know about "red beans and rice on Mondays" and sleeping under blankets monogrammed with SP (standing for Southern Pacific Railroad, where many of the men in our extended family worked) in the corners. I spent many a day at the free clinic getting shots and some pretty rugged dental care. I remember watching my mother and her friends gathering together to chop, mince, and stir the fixin's for the hog's head cheese, with its garlicky aroma and gelatinous texture that we got to taste with salted crackers the next day, after it had all been divvied up and slipped into cheesecloth packages for sharing. I know how grateful my mother and aunts were when the husbands who traveled the rails as porters came home with brown bags of filé (pronounced fee-lay) for gumbo that couldn't be found anywhere in this new West Coast territory we Creoles now called home. I know about collecting bottles to return for a few cents each in order to see the Saturday matinee. I'm aware of all that, but I scarcely have any memory at all of being *poor*.

Makes me wonder, what was different about that? Wonder if *poor* is a relative term that has little meaning if everyone in your world is at the same status? Maybe *poor* is a word that is always imposed externally, rarely recognized from *inside*. I suppose I must have had some sense of where we were on the economic scale by the time we were adolescents, but I'm not sure it was true even then. By that time we'd created our own criteria, and it included the uniqueness that comes with a Creole heritage. We were a proud people with standards that were considerably higher than many we lived among. We were just one more second-generation ethnic group, transplanted complete with the patois (at least among our elders), superstitions, folklore, songs, music, cuisine, and dimming memories of "home."

Poor?

Hell no! And envied by many for the gifts of jazz and good times that Creoles have brought to the world.

Rich beyond measure.

Though we must have been very poor financially, that is not what I remember. My world was nicely peopled with extended family. I weeded the garden with Papa George and got to choose the dinner vegetables that one of the female grown-ups prepared each day on the huge old woodstove that served to both feed us and keep us warm. I don't recall chopping the wood, but the job of stacking the box in the kitchen fell to us children. We also got to earn 25 cents for giving Papa his rare haircuts (he was bald with only a few wisps to trim), and it was always an honor to be chosen. Here in California, as in Ma-mair's house in New Orleans, there was the kerosene stove that sat in the middle of the room in winter.

The best of times were those after holiday parties had been staged at the Oakland Athletic Club, where Papa was a waiter. We'd be allowed to wait up for him to come home, no matter how late, and he would arrive like some jolly Santa with pockets bulging with whistles and horns, balloons, paper hats, and party foods for days!

When our uncles Herman, Lloyd, and Frederick would depart on their railroad runs, the grown-ups would walk with us out to the wetlands to stand beside the Southern Pacific tracks to wait for their train to go by. Our uncles would stand on the platform at the end of the train and toss out ice cream, packages of butter wrapped in towels, and sheets or an occasional gray blanket, or meats from the diner. It was a little like catching items from the floats at Mardi Gras, I suppose, and certainly not seen as a bad thing, since the conductor, who was white, was often seen standing beside our "tosser" and obviously approving. It was sheer delight! But that's a child's memory, of course. Maybe these were my earliest recollections of corporate power vs. the proletariat.

AT THE TIME we left Detroit and moved to New Orleans, my father was working in the automobile plant, I think at the Ford plant. He was a millwright. He was an architect by training. Not so much by education, just by training through his father.

What I've discovered in his family history is that in our line there was an arranged marriage back in the early 1800s, in which there was apparently unhappiness after one of the male members of the white side of the Charbonnet family took on a mulatto woman as his consort, or paramour, I guess it would be in French, with whom he fathered 11 children, one of whom was my great-grandfather, Dorson. Those 11 children, he educated very well. My grandfather, Louis, apparently became an engineer through correspondence courses at Tuskegee early on, and that was passed on to his children. So, to the extent that there was formal education, that was pretty high education in those days. I still have in my possession those textbooks that taught my grandfather.

Dorson Louis Charbonnet, my father, was tall, handsome, seemingly remote but soft and loving, formal. My dad wore a necktie to garden in. He was an aristocrat. And now I know why, in checking out the research of what went into that Charbonnet name for him. And I understand him better now than I did even then. I never saw him unless he was fully dressed. I don't think I ran into my dad in his pajamas until his last 10 years of life, when he was bedridden a good deal of the time.

I don't think my father, when I look back, I don't think he was ever comfortable with having three girls. Our relationship to him was very formal. He grew up with seven brothers, and there were several sisters, but my dad spoke rarely about his sisters, so I think that he was just not particularly comfortable with girls, because I remember him as a very formal being. I don't remember many intimate conversations with my father, though he was certainly loving and he did all the things a good father is supposed to do. I remember him only being playful in the context of being with other playful adults. I don't remember him being playful with us as children. But he was loving, and I did love him.

He did not come with us immediately when my mother and my sisters and I left New Orleans after the storm and moved to my grandfather's house in Oakland. He joined us two months later. I remember him at the time as a very handsome blue-eyed man, proud, who arrived in California just before the Depression hit with nothing, having lost everything in the hurricane—home, business. At first he could not get a job in California because he wasn't black enough for the railroads and he wasn't white enough to be white. He got a job at the Ford plant, but somebody reported to them that he was not white, that he was a black man passing, and he was fired. Smeone who was African American apparently told on him—you know this was dog-eat-dog days in the Depression, there were just no jobs. Then he got a job on the railroad wearing a white apron and for years was a lunch-car man.

After Dad joined us on the West Coast, the five of us Charbonnets left Papa George's and rented a tiny house on 76th Avenue just behind his, where we lived until I was about 10. Over those years, we watched from a distance as the airport slowly added hangars; watched the San Francisco Bay fill in until what the grown-ups called Depression Beach—a strip of sandy shore near the airport hangars—began to disappear. I wonder how we all survived those days when I remember that raw, untreated sewage was being pumped into the bay at that time. The odors on some days were almost unbearable. I suppose it had to do with the protective antibodies we'd built up over time, the kind that insure against all but the toughest bacteria! That may be why I've been so remarkably healthy all these years (smile).

Before my father ended his work life, he was able to get out of the manual labor he had been relegated to since coming to California and back to skilled work. I was in the process of moving out of my father and mother's household at the time, so I don't have a personal memory of these events, but my father told me later in life that he got a millwright job in the building of the Grosjean's Mill in San Francisco around 1940. As I said, my father was a millwright by trade, which is someone who takes a function and creates machinery to perform that function. The Albers Mill burned down on the Oakland waterfront in 1943—there was a huge fire—and they couldn't get anyone to rebuild that place. My dad told me later that he put together the design for the equipment that coated rice with Vitamin B, that whole process, and reestablished the conveyor belts at Albers. That was my dad's work.

He finally came back into his own, and one of the things that I was able to hand to my son David was Dad's union card—David, who eventually became a carpenter too. But Dad never again rose above the classification of carpenter, even though he was doing the work of a millwright, because of racism. But I think he never forgave anyone—and to this day, I think if he'd lived—that had he not left New Orleans he would have had, as his father did, a special status as a Creole.

OUR OAKLAND NEIGHBORHOOD was mixed racially. There were a number of black families. They had come to California from the South with a lot more race consciousness in a positive way, I think, than my parents and their group did. My parents had escaped that stuff and were glad to forget about it. And across the street there was a family that was also mulatto, like my family, but not Creole. My father would say they were "Americans." Then there were the Portuguese families and a few Irish families and Italian families that lived around the area.

So there was a life that was shared among the black families in our neighborhood. My dad and Mr. Dewson across the street, for example, the American non-Creole, would get together on weekends and play music. Dick Dewson played drums and Dad played piano, ragtime, and an old trumpet that he painted baby blue to plug up all the leaks. There was another man, too. There were three of them. They called themselves the Three Blind Mice.

Dad would wet his fingers and then he'd bump his spread fingers against the kitchen door in the rhythm of the music. And any of us who wanted to could be in the band, but you used comb and tissue paper or the pots and pans from the kitchen.

I knew almost intimately every single African American family in East Oakland. We all were one. A big band would come to town, to Sweet's Ballroom on Broadway in downtown Oakland, and they would hold what was called *dansans*, which were afternoon parties, and we would all go there to see Duke Ellington or Jimmie Lunceford and whoever it was who was playing, and every young person of color in the East Bay would be there. All of us would be in one place together. But this African American population during the time I was growing up must have not been more than ten or fifteen thousand people. In the entire Bay Area, that was it!

There were no strangers among the African American population in the East Bay at that time. But we were not separated out. We didn't have the sense of being separated out. Black people were together because they wanted to be. When the black baseball teams, the black leagues, came to town, we were all in the stands because we wanted to be, because black baseball was great!

But the life my parents shared with the non-Creole black people was not a social life. Our social life, my mother and father's social life, was Creole. The Creole families would come from throughout the Bay Area. They got together and they got their card tables and folding chairs and went on the streetcar to each other's houses. They planned lemonade parties for the children and kept us all together in a little group, so my social life was managed very much by my parents. We'd have roller-skating parties where we would start in East Oakland and skate downtown to Lake Merritt. I remember going to parties with my parents, because there were no such things as babysitters, and the kids would be thrown on a bed to sleep among the coats while the grown-ups partied in the next room. Our families—the Creole families—planned all these activities to keep these children together.

Many of these activities were Catholic-based. Catholicism is the predominant religion of Louisiana Creoles, and my family was very much Catholic.

My father remained a Catholic all his life. He was an official in the St. Vincent de Paul Society at St. Benedict's Church who counted the church collection, and he died a Catholic.

My mother died a Catholic, but a "cafeteria Catholic." She hardly went to church. I used to ask my mother how come she stayed in bed and we had to go to church. When I got old enough she told me, "I can't do this, because I believe in birth control, but some things are none of the priest's business." My mother was practicing birth control. She only had three children, and she had to choose between her sexuality and her religion, and I think my mother chose her sexuality. So she could not receive the sacraments. But my father was active in the church because he didn't have to bear that sin.

I can't remember intellectually thinking my way out of Catholicism, but sort of flunking Catholicism. I think if I'd been a good Catholic I would have wound up a nun, because I was a purist as a kid. I think about that now—that if I really had believed, I'd have gone pretty far and pretty deep into it, but somewhere early on, somewhere maybe even as early as 11 or 12, it began to not ring true for me. It was a place where I became more fascinated with questions than answers, because for me at that point, all of the growth was happening in the area of questions. The answers provided by the people around me didn't suffice, and it was not that I thought they were wrong as much as that I think at a very early age I became aware of how much there was to be known. That became a handicap for me, because the people around me *knew*.

One thing the Creoles didn't bring with them from Louisiana to California was the Mardi Gras celebrations. It was not picked up. It was not celebrated. But they did bring with them all of the post–Mardi Gras Lent and Easter rituals. I remember the novenas during Lent. From a very, very early age, I remember my entire family being involved in the Catholic rituals of Lent and Good Friday and Easter. I remember my mother's set getting together the night before Ash Wednesday, I guess it was Shrove Tuesday, the last night of the Mardi Gras season, and the women would get together to make headcheese, which was one of the meals for those observances. I don't remember them making it any other time during the year.

EVEN THOUGH I HAD a very active social life among both the Creole families and the black families growing up, I also had a solitary life.

There were three girls in our family—Margie, the oldest; myself, and Lottie. And we were each spaced out so that we were four years apart. I don't remember sharing much life with them, because we were never in the same schools at the same time. We were never in the same social groups at the same time. We didn't really share much life until we got to be adults. By that time I think it was too late; we didn't forge close relationships, because my eldest sister married when she was 19, which means that I was 15. So she went out of my life and into her own and I became the oldest. And then when I was married at 20, my younger sister was only 15.

So I moved out into my own life. And as we became nuclear families of our own, we didn't reconnect. My sense of us as adults is that we were all pretty much strangers. Marjorie moved to Southern California, then to Kansas for a long time, because her husband was with one of the black insurance companies. Then they moved back to Southern California, which is where they raised their children. My younger sister also moved around a good deal more than I did. And I moved out into the suburbs. So we disconnected early. I wish that we had had more time together. My own kids were spaced closer, and I think I did that consciously.

I must have been withdrawn as a little kid. And I remember being very, very thin. I didn't weigh a hundred pounds until I was 50. My parents were very small-boned, little people. Dad was tall at six feet, but he was slender always. So it was genetic. But I remember spending a lot of time in county clinics. The county referred me there.

I was away for a year in a preventorium in Livermore, which is out in the valley several miles from Oakland. This was a place for children who might be at high risk for tuberculosis. My father had tuberculosis at one point, so they sent me out there, where I spent a year. That was when I was 12 or 13.

I can close my eyes and remember it. I can remember being on some sort of deck and wearing loincloths and laying in the sun, because every day we had to toast ourselves on one side and then the other.

The discussion between my parents to send me away to the Arroyo Del Valle preventorium was probably held in French so I wouldn't know what was coming. I simply was gathered up and taken there for my own good. I remember being just terribly disturbed by it for a while. When I came back home after a year at the preventorium I felt like I was coming into a nest of strangers. It took me a long time to get back into the fold. In some respects, I never did.

Del Valle was another place where I got disconnected from family and was just absolutely, just totally isolated, because my parents couldn't get out there to see me very often, only every couple of months. I was a lonely little girl in a strange setting very far away from home. I can remember doing a lot of reading.

Reading was a big thing for me. I read a great deal as a child. I remember as a very little kid reading my way through the Ruth Fielding series of books—a series of girls' stories. Then I went into poetry. I loved Edna St. Vincent Millay. When I was 11 or 12 I would sing "Renascence." I mean, I loved it. That's when I began to use music. I would read poetry and then wonder how this would sound if notes were added, and then I would add those notes and sing it. All of this was in a very isolated life of a little girl. I don't remember doing this with anyone.

I remember actually meeting James Baldwin at a reading at a local church at one point and hearing him read his work. That was when I must have been in my late teens or a young adult. But I was not introduced to black writers until I was an adult. In fact, I had never even heard James Weldon Johnson's great Negro national anthem, "Lift Ev'ry Voice and Sing," and I remember hearing it for the first time and thinking it was subversive. How could this be? I'd never met people who had attended Southern schools except my Aunt Vivian, but she and I did not talk about those things.

MY BEST FRIEND during my early years in Oakland was my grandfather, Papa George. He was a waiter at the Oakland Athletic Club. His best friend was his brother-in-law, Joe Warnie, who we called Daddy Joe. These two old friends played penny ante and pinochle every Saturday night of their lives.

I would go with Papa every Saturday evening to the Warnies' home and would play with my cousins in their shared attic bedroom as he and Daddy Joe played their card games far into the night in the kitchen below.

When it wasn't baseball season, they would play a little longer into Sunday morning, because on those days Papa could get his rest on Sunday afternoons. But if the traveling barnstormers were in town, the card games would end at a more reasonable hour, and Papa and I would head out to San Pablo Park in Berkeley to see the games as soon as church was out. Papa was hardly a churchgoer, but he did respect Sunday morning church hours as inviolate, as did all of the grown-ups in my life. Fun had to wait until one's spiritual duties had been performed, even if they were performed in absentia.

On baseball Sundays, I would ride across town to the park with Papa in the stalwart Model T that was durable but failing in the later years. He called it a *flivver*, and it was a terrible little Ford.

I sat beside him, ever ready to slide into the driver's seat when she'd die at the stop signs and have to be cranked. He would remove his coat and jump out with the crank, and I would sit and push the spark—a little lever attached to the steering column—when signaled to do so by my grandfather.

We'd stop and start all the way across town from 75th Avenue in East Oakland to 29th Street in North Oakland, or then to San Pablo Park in Berkeley for the games. We were a pretty good team, actually, and always managed to get there, so even in those early years I developed a sense of being capable, much needed, and useful. Papa always treated me as an equal, and I was, at least in handling our transportation problems. I don't recall ever being either embarrassed or impatient at such times; the stalled times were simply part of the adventure, and Papa's constant patter and sometimes-ribald stories were such fun. Not sure that my mother would have approved, had she known, but these were private conversations that I knew were to be kept so.

He was the adult in my life. He may not have been the world's most accomplished male, and he was kind of a scandalous character, according to my mother. She was very embarrassed by him. They didn't have a good relationship. He was very close to her younger sister, Vivian, but that may have come from the fact that my mother was sort of abandoned to my grandmother as a baby, and then he brought back these other children from another marriage and they never really reestablished a relationship.

I heard that my grandfather was a womanizer of the worst kind. I only knew that filtered through my mother's prejudices. When he was in his 80s and his third wife had died, he was rumored to be supporting some woman across town on his pension, and my mother's younger sister, Vivian, was supporting him in this life of sin. I don't know now whether that was anything or not, except that he always had a wink in his eye and he was always somebody I was a little apprehensive around. But it never did turn me off enough to back away from him, because he was my grown-up friend.

He was a playful man. I remember working in his truck garden out on 76th Avenue and digging in the soil with him, and he was always singing little funny songs that I now recognize as the kind of blues and folk things that had come out on record from Lightnin' Hopkins and Jimmy McCracklin and people like that. I remember my grandfather as singing these little songs that had no meaning anywhere outside the context of that gardening thing that we did together. I didn't hear his songs on the radio, for instance.

I ATTENDED HIGH SCHOOL at Castlemont High in East Oakland. I was aware of racial prejudice when I was in high school. That's when it really began to dawn on me that we were separate people. It came to me through classes that I took, it came to me through my parents.

Around the time when one decides on studying a foreign language in school, I went to my mother and told her I wanted to take French, because the older people in the family spoke French, and this would let me into the club. I'd never been able to really know what the family gossip was because the older members would drop into French or Creole as soon as they didn't want us kids to hear. And my mother said, "No, you look more Spanish. You need to take Spanish." That's because I was darker than my two sisters, and there was a certain amount of shame connected with dark skin. That was the beginning, when I began to sense the limitations that were placed on me. There was a suggestion that I was going to have to pass if I was going to do anything of importance. That was the first hint. So I took Spanish.

Some of it was Creole pride, pride just in being Creole, and I'm appreciating that more now. But part of it was just the same kind of racism that I saw outside. It took me a long time to forgive them for that.

I remember my mother, for example, saying unforgivable things, such as looking at one now well-known, accomplished woman in my age group and saying, "Those parents sure better educate that girl, because she'll never get a husband." Education was second to physical attractiveness, always.

But then, of course, there was the greater racism of the larger community in which our Creole and black communities lived.

When I went to high school at Castlemont, for instance, there were only, I think, three or four black kids in the entire school. My sister Marjorie was one of the first black kids to attend Castlemont, if you can believe that!

I remember being in the drama class, and I must have been about a sophomore, a junior, maybe, and we were reading Maxwell Anderson's *Winterset*. I was reading for the part of Mariamne, and I knew I had done well. But when we were finished, my teacher held me after class. She said to me, "You did a very good job in that role, but you know I can't give it to you. You can't play that part against Eddie Castro. Eddie's white, and the parents would never allow that."

I had a sense of being guilty for bringing this problem to her. I felt I was inconveniencing everybody, and there was a certain amount of shame mixed in with the hurt of rejection that's very different from what kids have to deal with now.

But I also had a retreat into my own social group. When I got into high school, there were things I didn't do partly because of fear of being isolated by the few black kids that were there, because I was lighter-skinned, and you don't want to put your neck out too far because you need real friends. And not really feeling like a part of white high school social life, because my social life was being taken care of outside of it. And if anything, I felt superior.

The kids that I was going to parties with on weekends, our boyfriends were at San Jose State, they were at Cal. I was dating men like Kenny Washington from UCLA, who was their big quarterback, and Jackie Robinson, all these people. We were among the celebrity group as long as we were black, so we were black by choice. We were going to the International House near the UC Berkeley campus for parties and formal dances. I didn't go to my senior ball, there would have been nothing there for me. I was going with the kids at sororities and the fraternities at Cal. My contemporaries at school were going with the guy who worked at the gas station around the corner. The white kids were lower-class white kids, while the black kids were part of an elite group. So that played against that trend of black feelings of inferiority.

I went to my junior prom, which was very disillusioning. It was the first time I had ever attended a social event where everybody was white but me. And before the evening was over, everybody was drunk. That had never been true in my world. In my world, people held debut parties when they turned 18. We were highly socialized. If anything, I thought we were snobs.

Academically, there was a teacher in high school in public speaking who did tremendous things for me. I remember him lighting up when I got up to contribute. He was a wonderful, wonderful teacher. He would ask challenging questions.

To this day, I can remember a long debate about euthanasia in that public speaking class, and I can remember that the kids went off, as people do, into the fine line between euthanasia and murder and people being eliminated. I remember raising my hand and waving it around trying to get his attention and having him ignore me for a long time and knowing that he knew that I knew, but it wasn't time yet to let this into the room. I guess I was a sophomore at the time, but I can remember having a sense of being on the same level with this teacher, because somehow we both knew that I knew. Also that I was cooperating with his game about not saying it yet. And finally toward the end of the discussion, I remember having him point to me so I could say, "But you're no longer talking about euthanasia, you're talking about murder," and having him say, "Aha." And having this sense for the first time of being at an adult intellectual level and how freeing this was for a kid.

He introduced me to all kinds of concepts that were beyond the limitations that I was facing in other classes. He's probably the only teacher besides my drama teacher that I really remember now. We were often going to New Orleans to visit the family during these times, and I remember coming back and not being pressed, because I never had to work in high school. I wonder sometimes what I could have accomplished if I'd ever been challenged in high school, because I wasn't in any way. I bounced through high school because no one ever asked for a report card. I always signed my own. My parents never participated when I was in school in any way. They were satisfied that I was going, and that was it. I was a good girl, so no one had to deal with me in any way. I was not a problem. So I sort of blandly went through school without being challenged at all.

The other children in school were on college tracks. But those kids were all white and that was not within the realm of possibility for me. So I was on a track for commercial training, typing and that sort of stuff. I could do that stuff with my hand tied behind my back. That's where I was supposed to be, and I can't remember resisting this at the time.

I MET MY FIRST HUSBAND, Mel, when I was 13. He lived around the corner from San Pablo Park in Berkeley. We met at a baseball game where he came and he was on his bicycle and delivering papers. I was there watching the baseball game with Papa George.

At that time, San Pablo Park was one of the centers of social activities for the black community. There were tennis leagues, and the black baseball leagues—called the colored leagues then—played there.

Mel's ambition was to become two things, because the limitations on where blacks could go and what blacks could do were pretty well understood. He wanted to be a bakery wagon driver and work at Wonder Bread, where his father worked. But that was a union job and the unions weren't accepting any non-white workers at the time, so he was outside that. And he wanted to be a playground director. That was also a white job at the time.

Mel's father, Tom Reid, could never be in the union. Tom's job at the bakery was unloading 100-pound flour sacks from the railcars and carrying them to the dock. He started when he was about 14 or 15, retired still doing the same thing, loading 100-pound flour sacks from the railcars to the docks. Because that's all a black man could do at the time.

But Mel later did become the playground director at San Pablo Park.

Mel was a great athlete at Berkeley High School. From there he went to Sacramento State and then to the University of San Francisco. He went to college on a football scholarship. He was All-State, All-Star, all-everything—an all-star when he was in high school and in college. After college he became a player with the California Golden Eagles, who were part of the black baseball leagues. He also played for the Oakland Giants, which was the first pro football team in Oakland before the National Football League was organized. He played for the Hawaiian Warriors for some time professionally, but that was before the big leagues were actually formed. He was a very, very well-known athlete.

I didn't realize the specialness of Mel's family until I began to meet some of the younger members of his family who were into history. I knew that Mel's family had been here for a great many years, but I had no idea what that meant. His predecessors were out of Virginia and Georgia, and some of them had relocated to California before the Civil War. Some of them were founding members of the Third Baptist Church in San Francisco, which is one of the oldest and most important black churches on the West Coast.

One of Mel's great-great-grandfathers, William Henry Galt, was a captain in the Sacramento Zouaves, the black militia unit that was part of the organized state effort during the Civil War to keep California in the Union and out of the Confederacy. And one of Mel's great-grandfathers, Edward Parker, was one of the first black people to register to vote in California as soon as it was allowed, in 1870.

Another one of Mel's relatives was William Patterson, who was the attorney who wrote up the famous "We Charge Genocide" petition that Paul Robeson presented before the United Nations in 1951. Patterson was a mentor to Robeson. He later wrote an autobiography, also called *We Charge Genocide*, which includes information about his and Mel's family history in Virginia and how they came to California. Patterson was a member of the Communist Party USA and went to Russia with Paul Robeson when Robeson visited the Soviet country. Unfortunately, Mel's family was very ashamed of him for this, and nobody spoke about him. But I find him a great source of pride.

3

MARRIAGE AND THE WAR YEARS

GOING THROUGH OLD FILE drawers recently in the hope of parting with more old records, and there, beneath the clutter, laid a silver half-dollar. It looked strange, as if from some other nation and some other time, but as I held it in the palm of my hand, unexpected tears welled up and memories came flooding back of what I now recognize as the very first political act of an impressionable young Betty on her first job.

I'd just graduated from Castlemont High in Oakland and was about to be launched out into the working world of domestics. A friend of my mother's had passed along a referral for a job with a white family who were moving into a home just off Seminary Avenue in East Oakland in the shadow of Mills College and wanted to hire a "girl" for the weekend to help in that process. This would be my first job and I was ready, though I had no idea what it meant, except that this was the very first step into my future (until I could marry, of course).

I appeared on the job early on Friday morning with the understanding that I would spend the next two days living in and working with this mother as she prepared the house for occupancy. It meant scouring the two bathrooms as well as the kitchen on my hands and knees with scrub brush, sponge, and bucket and washing shelves and lining them with paper in preparation for unpacking endless cardboard cartons of dishes, pots and pans, glasses, etc., throughout Friday and all of Saturday.

At the end of each day I helped to prepare dinner for the woman and her husband plus three children. On Saturday evening the parents took off for a movie, so I was expected to manage the kids and get them bathed and into bed by 8:30 before falling onto a cot in one of the children's rooms, exhausted, until morning.

On Sunday morning I helped with breakfast and washed and dried the dishes before helping to get the children dressed for church. I then went back to the shared bedroom to listen to a radio until the family was scheduled to return at around noontime.

I heard the car drive into the garage and waited anxiously for my time to end so I could return home with my first earnings in hand. There had been no agreement as to just what those earnings might consist of, but I knew that my mother had mentioned something about "50 cents an hour," and I'd envisioned this windfall and spent it on many things as I washed and dried dishes, wiped kids' noses, and anticipated wildly.

My employer came to me as I sat at the kitchen table with my coat over my arm, ready to leave. Into my outstretched palm she slipped a half-dollar with the words "I wish it could be more, dear, but you know you are really not an experienced helper . . ." Her voice trailed off, as I remember, but maybe I'm just remembering my own inability to comprehend what this meant.

I said nothing. Gathered up my things and left this house to catch the bus at the corner store, all the while struggling to understand what had happened. I held the silver coin in my palm tightly as the bus meandered its way through the familiar neighborhood. When I rose to pull the cord that signaled my stop, I left the half dollar on the seat, got off the bus and walked the half block to our home, streaming tears of crushing disappointment!

This was my only experience as a domestic.

There were three choices open to young women of color in those days: (1) working in agriculture, (2) being a domestic servant, or (3) marrying well. I skipped the first and briefly took the second. Within a year or so, I'd taken the third choice.

MEL WAS AS LOCKED into his role as I was in mine, my ambition to be a young married woman with a husband and a child and having this prescribed life. On his side, he felt the obligation to be a provider, to take care of a wife and children. When we got married, he had worked when he was in school with his paper route and he would assist his father sometimes on weekends to be able to support a wife and family. Mel was an accomplished guy. He had saved his money for getting married. He had enough money saved up to put a down payment on a little duplex on Sacramento Street. The whole cost of that duplex was, I think, $4,500, and the down payment was $750 or something of that sort. At that time salaries were almost nothing, so it's all relative. But at any rate, as a young couple we moved into a place that we were buying.

We didn't have a honeymoon. We went home to our own place after the wedding.

We got very busy being husband and wife and getting ready to produce children—that was our role.

When Mel and I married I was 20 and didn't have a job, because at that time that choice wasn't open to women. You married and then you had your child, and I was a complete failure when I had been married three years and had not yet given birth. I think it's interesting that my younger sister and my older sister—who were by now both married, because my four-years-younger sister married at 17 and my four-years-older sister married at 19—were both pregnant, and I was not. I'd not done my job, I'd not fulfilled my role as a young married woman.

Now when I look back, that really says a lot about the milieu in which I grew up, and the way those rules were laid down and how demanding they were. But at that point there was no choice. I was married in May of 1942, the war started in 1941. Mel was working at the shipyard and then enlisted in the Navy. I was at home and I was supposed to support my husband in what he wanted to do. That was my role.

But then I had no children, and Mel was very, very disappointed that we had not had kids. And he was really pressing hard, and I thought it was a physical failure on my part that I was barren. I had imagined that 15 minutes after I was married I was going to get pregnant and then have a baby nine months later, and this just didn't happen. So at that time, I just saw myself as sterile, so I was sort of allowed to do other things. So I went to work.

THE FIRST JOB I worked at was in San Francisco in the Civil Service Commission in the basement of the federal building. The war was already on.

My job at that time was as a file clerk, in the "flagging" section. You'd go in the morning and pick up a tray of pink and blue cards with the names of individuals on them who had taken civil service examinations. Then you'd sit at long tables with lots of other people with what were called bar-and-flag files. Each of these files would have findings that would demand barring and flagging of people. Flagging—the blue cards—meant look further before you hire them for a government job; barring—the pink cards— meant they could not work for the federal government under any circumstances: either they couldn't get the job they were seeking, or they were fired from a job they already had. I didn't even wonder about the genesis of that stuff, because I wasn't sophisticated enough. It was a job and I was filing cards.

You didn't get a card filed in this department until you applied for a position in either the shipyards or one of the war plants. Of course, just about the entire Bay Area was war plants at the time, and people were not hired or were fired for all these reasons that they would never know.

You'd have to sign a loyalty oath to work in the shipyards, to work at any defense plant, which meant that you'd have to swear not to work for anything that would overthrow the government, so that was the reason that they could throw you out.

When I read the cards they would talk about things like "car license plate read within a block of known communist cell meeting," that sort of thing. So this had to be FBI stuff. But I didn't really know what the FBI was; why would I even know that?

But I finally saw a card, a flag card, bearing the name of my brother-in-law, my sister's husband, who was working in the ship-yards at Mare Island in Vallejo and whose car was seen parked within a block of a known communist cell meeting, or a suspected communist cell meeting. But I knew my brother-in-law was in no way a communist, so at that point I became more interested in these cards and what they said. I began to find other people that I knew who had applied for work but were barred or flagged. That was the beginning of my awareness. I began to get aware of this level of government, that there was something here that I did not know about and had no reason to be aware of until I had that job.

At that time we were experiencing blackouts and air-raid warnings with some frequency, and my parents were concerned about my being caught in San Francisco with no way to get home, so it became necessary that I seek work on the east side of the bay, where we lived. So after a while I transferred from the Civil Service Commission into the Air Force because it was an easy transfer, because I was already sworn in as a federal employee.

When I went to work there, I got to be close friends with a young white girl whose desk was facing mine. But I also ran into a friend who was African American, about my color, who looked like me, who was a part of my social group. I saw her several times, but each time I saw her she ducked away from me.

She had been a former fiancée of Mel's, so I didn't know whether she was being distant because of that or what it was. But one day we met together in the restroom for the first time and there was nowhere for her to go, and she asked me what I was passing for. I said, "Nothing." And she said, "You have to be, because you can't work here if you're colored." It turned out that *she* was passing for white. And I realized then that no one had bothered to tell anyone at the new job that I wasn't white because I was a direct transfer.

Then I became apprehensive because I was suddenly passing for white and didn't know it. A day or two afterward, the young woman whose desk abutted mine was called up to the lieutenant in charge of our section, and I saw her shaking her head and nodding and her face reddened as they talked. Her discomfort was visible even from the distance between us. My sixth sense told me that someone had reported me.

Mind you, I'd never passed in my life. There was all the shame that was connected with having to do something I wouldn't have done if I'd had a choice. Because this was not a problem for me, my race may have been their problem, but it wasn't mine. It had never had to be. So here I was in this awkward, unanticipated position.

So, when she got back to our work area I asked her what was that about and she kept her face down and wouldn't look at me directly. I said, "They found out that I'm not white?" and she said, "Yes, but don't worry, because I told them it's not a problem." So I said, "But it's a problem for me." So I got up and I walked the length of that room and I got to the lieutenant's desk and I said, "Who told you that I was what I was? I didn't tell you I was white, because I came here and didn't fill out an application. I came here as a transfer. Didn't you know that I was colored?" Clearly nervous and embarrassed, he said, "Don't worry, don't worry, I'm told that it's not a problem, that you're okay, that you can stay. Everyone here is willing to work with you." I mean, think about that: "Everyone here is willing to work with you."

I said, "But are they willing to work under me? I'm in line for an upgrade." And he said, "You'll receive your level pay raises," but it was clear that my status was not going to be raised, I was not going to be upgraded and put in charge of other workers, so I walked out on the U.S. government and told them to shove it, and that was the end of that.

Meanwhile, Mel had enlisted in the Navy. And two days after I walked out of my job with the Air Force, he came back home, having refused to go into the messmen's corps and be a cook. He was a proud, accomplished, well-known, and celebrated athlete who was in his senior year at the University of San Francisco. He had wanted to be a full seaman with regular duties, but all of the blacks who were in the Navy at the time were being sent to the

Navy's Great Lakes base to be trained as cooks. And Mel wouldn't do it, so they told him that they would have to send him home. Refusal to serve was almost unheard of at that time, and he never got over the shame of it.

The Navy presented him with a check for $45 in mustering-out pay and released him without prejudice. They presented him with an honorable discharge. The examining officer, a psychiatrist, asked him why he hadn't come in as a white man because he was light-skinned for a Negro and could have avoided all this. He added, "We don't doubt that you would make an exemplary naval man, Reid, but we simply can't afford to put a man like you—a natural leader of men—on shipboard with men who might be easily led. That could spell mutiny at sea."

For Mel, who had never had to pass, and for whom his race was part of his pride, it was an unforgivable insult. Upon returning home to Berkeley, he went back to the shipyards, because there were lots of other blacks there. He also worked as a playground director in a multiracial community, where his race didn't matter.

That is when we decided that as soon as we could, we were not going to work for anybody, we were going to go into business for ourselves, because the whole field had become muddied for us at that point and we didn't want any part of it. The World War II experience was really a coming-of-age thing for us both, racially. And we had to choose. We had to choose an identity.

BUT UNTIL WE WERE able to start a business of our own, we still had to work. So I went to work in Richmond as a clerk for Auxiliary Lodge Number 36 (A-36) of the International Brotherhood of Boilermakers, Iron Ship Builders, and Helpers of America. The Boilermakers union had previously been all-white, but with the coming of World War II there was a shortage of white men to fill the new jobs opening up in the war effort, and they began to bring blacks into the trade. But instead of bringing them into the main union local, they set up a separate local that was just for the black workers coming in. And that was auxiliary number A-36. Black men were hired starting in 1943 to do the heavy lifting for the women who had been hired. All of them were hired as helpers and trainees only, never to go above those classifications.

At the time, I wasn't aware of the history of the auxiliary and how it came to be formed. I was just filing cards again, the same kind of no-brain work that I had done at the Civil Service Commission.

I was aware that it was African American, and I was very aware that we were working toward the war effort, but I don't remember that as being exceptional. It was part of all the chaos that was going on. I had watched the people literally coming in, watched the trains as they passed in front of my house, loaded with people coming into the Bay Area. And defense work was an important thing. But I don't remember feeling particularly patriotic in that job; that wasn't what it was about. I did feel that being clerical was a step up from being a housemaid, and, as such, I had attained something to be proud of. Most of our mothers and aunts were domestics doing "day work," taking care of white people's homes, tending white people's children, making beds in hotels, emptying bedpans in the rest homes and hospitals. Our fathers and our uncles were Pullman porters, cooks, waiters, janitors, laborers, bellhops, barbers, shoe shiners, elevator operators—all service workers. So I was doing clerical work, which was seen as a baby-step up, almost the equivalent of today's young woman of color being the first in her family to enter college. That's who we were as a nation in the year 1942.

And though we were hiring and representing workers at the Richmond shipyards, I never saw a ship under construction nor a ship launching. I wasn't even aware of them. We were encapsulated in this one little temporary building somewhere in the middle of the city, nowhere near the shoreline.

The camaraderie among the workers is what made that job important to me, and it's the only thing I really remember about it. I don't remember protests. I don't remember resentments. I don't remember anyone talking about the fact that it was a black union. I don't remember the political parts of that at all. I was not aware of it. It fit the times that we were getting through, and so it was okay.

It wasn't until years later that I became resentful about the situation and began to resist the inequities as I lived them.

The local United Service Organizations— the USOs—were segregated and did not entertain African American servicepeople. So Mel and I and other local black residents entertained the servicemen—from Port Chicago, from Camp Stoneman, from Camp Ashby—in our homes. This was largely innocent lemonade parties on Saturday afternoons. We were sort of their home away from home. This was common to all the families, the African American families, who felt this camaraderie with the African American servicepeople.

Over time Mel began to bring home small groups of servicemen who used to gather at San Pablo Park, where Mel worked, so the servicemen could meet our friends and neighbors for informal hours of small talk and lemonade.

One particular afternoon, there must've been maybe a dozen or so young sailors from Port Chicago weapons station, about 20 miles away. We were dancing to records and swapping tales for a few hours before they hit their curfew and had to make the trip back to their base for the grim routine of loading ammunition for the battles raging in the South Pacific.

I remember that they left just before dark to avoid traveling in the dim-out back to their base. The explosion happened about 10:30 and we were not yet asleep. And we didn't recognize it as an explosion at first, thought maybe it was a bombing by the Japanese or that there was an earthquake, because we lived in earthquake country. It wouldn't become clear until the morning news, when the announcement came that there'd been an explosion at Port Chicago in which two ships were lost. The tremor measured on the Richter scale as far away as Reno.

There was this young sailor named Richert from Mississippi I had been talking to, and the reason I remember him was because he looked white, and people questioned his being there. For the first hour or so, they didn't know what he was doing there because he was obviously an outsider. And he had to defend his status as a person of color. And I don't recall what the conversation was between us, except that we learned in that conversation that he was only 16. He had lied about his age to get into the service. And he was the one, probably because of his age, that I have continued to worry about all these years, as to what was his fate. His name does not appear on the memorial. So he has continued to be an enigma to me, unless I allow myself to think about the possibility that Richert was one of the unknowns, mixed in among the body parts that were gathered up in 24 caskets and buried in the colored section at Golden Gate National Cemetery in San Bruno, California, after the explosion.

That scar has continued to live with me, because I never knew what happened to Richert. And I don't know if any of the other servicemen at our party were among those killed in the explosion, because I didn't know the names of any of the others who had been with us that afternoon.

WHEN MEL AND I first got married, we lived in a small duplex on Sacramento Street in Berkeley. The reason that's important is that down Sacramento Street ran the Santa Fe rail line, in the middle of our street, so the home front was playing itself out right in front of my door. Day and night, there were huge, long trains of people being brought in—mostly from the five Southern states—for work in the shipyards. Hanging out of the windows—because at that time, the windows weren't sealed in trains—leaning out of the vestibules, waving, getting their first view of California and the Bay Area. And we were sort of the welcome committee, all along our street. We would wave people into California.

Coming in by the thousands on these loaded trains, passed in front of our door, day after day, day and night, hundreds of thousands of people coming in. Henry Kaiser alone imported 98,000 black and white Southerners for his four Richmond shipyards, all of them pouring into the town of Richmond, which had only held a total population of 23,000.

The movement in the community was a physical thing for me. I was watching this happen and people fanning out, I was watching the construction of the war housing to warehouse these people.

Talk about earthquakes! Human quakes were going on in every way, the change from 1942 or 1941, in the beginning of the war and into the '60s, that 20 years, how many times did California's population turn over? It was like living in four different states without ever leaving home, because the rate of change was so great and the changes in our own lives were so great. The world was literally changing around us, just so fast that there was no way we could keep up.

When we were growing up, the social levels were not based upon money or degrees. Our fathers were the barbers and redcaps and carpenters, laborers, waiters—service workers, all—and we were together because of the fact that we were all colored, and that was it. But now, following the migration of lots and lots of other people, there was a professional class that also came in. There were suddenly a lot more professional blacks who were also living here. Suddenly there were doctors and dentists, pharmacists, attorneys, and people to service the incoming black community, and our group became somewhat irrelevant and buried under this new class of people.

I look back now and I don't know how we survived it, except that it was like an avalanche. Our little community, our little colored community, was just buried under an avalanche of people, strangers, not necessarily black and white, but strangers. Our community physically changed within a matter of months. It's like we'd moved out of the state into another state without even leaving home, so it was just unbelievable.

I didn't have friends among the newcomers. But I don't think we had enough time to develop a tension between the newcomers and the old-timers, particularly. I don't remember there being hostility between us, because there were a lot more of them than there were of us, and I think there would have been not that much consciousness among the newcomers that there were even people like us already here. And we were all busy with the war effort. There was this bigger thing outside all of us. We were all living under the common threat of Fascist world domination.

THE LITTLE DUPLEX that Mel and I bought when we got married had been owned by a man named Aldo Musso, who had a jukebox route. He was very fond of Mel, and he got Mel to help him service the boxes. Mr. Russo would pay him to go around and change the records in these boxes, which is how Mel discovered that whole industry. Mel found how hard it was to find the music to put into the fast-developing black clubs and restaurants, all the little sandwich shops that were beginning to pop up—there was no way to get them. That was the way Mel started off. That was the door that opened up the whole idea of putting together a shop of his own.

We opened up by parking our car on the street and turning the garage of our little duplex into a makeshift shop, with orange crates holding the records and albums and a wooden box for a cash register. That's around the same time we adopted Rick. He was born in March, we opened the store in June of the same year. So I had a bassinet and little playpen down near the cash register. I sold records through a window roughly cut into the garage wall while Mel was at the shipyards and doing his other things, which included semi-pro baseball and professional football when in season, and working at San Pablo Park as an assistant recreation director and coach.

KRE was a local radio station that had some pretty hip disc jockeys. There were no black jocks at all, but they were excited by the music we presented them with, and they began to play it. We put on the first commercial spot we had with Wynonie Harris doing "Around the Clock." It would be nothing in today's music world, but it was really risqué for us at that time, it was really over the edge. It was filled with innuendo, sexual innuendo. And after KRE started playing it on the air and advertising our shop, people would literally come down and they could hardly find the place because it was so tiny and almost hidden in this garage, but they would circle the block until they found it, trying to buy this record. And that's when we found out how big black music really was.

The black community was our first customers, and a certain number of whites who were logging into the black blues at that time. We became very, very well known in the local music world. We weren't into gospel at all at first. Eventually we became only a gospel store, but up until then it was all blues, jazz, and R&B, artists like Lou Rawls and Lightnin' Hopkins, Billie Holiday, Dinah Washington, Louis Jordan, Slim Gaillard, Jimmie Lunceford, Duke Ellington, and Erskine Hawkins. That kind of jazz was really big.

I was certainly a Duke Ellington fan, totally for years and years, still am. I loved Sarah Vaughn, but that was in her beginning, way, way back. I loved Billie Holiday, but not as much in the beginning as later. I could not relate to traditional black blues for a long, long time. I was a jazz buff always. I would move along with jazz as jazz developed and changed and could go with it, but that wasn't true for me with blues. Later, much later, when I came back into the business, the day came when I knew that the best jazz was coming out of the choir loft. I recognized contemporary black gospel as "jazz come home." This was something that I can only now fully appreciate.

I was sort of everything in the beginning at the shop, because Mel had two other jobs. I did it all. I was behind the counter, I organized the stock and did the ordering and did the shipping, wrote a mimeographed newsletter that eventually reached even overseas to servicemen and -women serving in the Korean War, with a print run of 20,000. That little newsletter ended only when the business could no longer afford the postage to mail it out! But it was through that mimeographed newsletter that I first found my political voice.

We eventually had three small stores, the original one in Berkeley, one in Swann's Market, which was in downtown Oakland, and one in Vallejo, small shops.

It was around the time that we opened the downtown Oakland store that Mel's Uncle Paul joined the business. Paul Reid had been a really fine salesman with the black-owned Golden State Mutual Life Insurance Company, which was a black insurance company. He left there and joined Mel in the business, and that's when things really took off because he had a lot of know-how. He was the public part of Reid's. I have some pictures around here with Paul. He emceed concerts. They gave huge concerts, choir competitions throughout the Bay Area. They filled the Oakland Auditorium, which held upward of 6,000 people, absolutely filled it. And Mel grew to be a very, very important promoter himself.

After Paul joined the business, the store began to shift its inventory to gospel. Paul was a churchman. He was the member of the Reid's Records team who sort of brought that out. He and Mel brought in black gospel performers from around the country. James Cleveland out of Los Angeles, Shirley Caesar and the Caravans, the Five Blind Boys of Mississippi, the Staple Singers, the Clark Sisters, Aretha Franklin's father, Reverend C. L. Franklin. They were the big gospel stars of the time, and they were all brought into the Bay Area for concerts, *huge* concerts.

But I was not involved by that time. That was pretty much after I had stopped working at the store and was at home raising kids out in the suburbs of the East Bay.

IN KEEPING WITH MY "good girl" profile, and having fulfilled the strong wishes of my parents, I fully expected to bear my first child nine months and 24 hours after the wedding ceremony. Not so. My older sister, Marjorie, had been married for five years and was pregnant with her second child, and my youngest sister, Lottie, who was four years younger, had married at 17 and was expecting her first. I had been, up to that point, unable to conceive. In my early 20s, having two sisters pregnant and feeling barren, I started to explore adoption.

Mel was less than enthusiastic. That was during the time when he was first making plans for the record business, where I was slated to be the on-site "employee," and he was still active in his sports career, with thoughts of taking that to a higher level as some black professional athletes were doing, so he considered my desire for parenthood for the two of us through adoption to be an impediment to his own ambitions.

But I'd waited impatiently for motherhood to begin and saw his plans as further postponement of my own dreams. Catholic Social Services announced in January that a child would be available in a month or so, and in March of that year, 1945, Dale Richard Reid, a nine-day-old little boy, was ours.

Marjorie's son, Lottie's daughter, and Rick all came into the world over a three-month period. The Charbonnet girls had delivered on cue.

Thankfully, it took only a few hours for Mel to bond with our baby. He was a loving father. My gratitude for his having yielded to my wishes gave me a feeling of indebtedness that hemmed me in and defined my life for many years. I actually loved mothering. I got a real thrill out of being a parent. But at the same time, I also dedicated myself to making real Mel's dream of owning his own business as payment for a debt I owned to him for allowing me fulfillment of my maternal role in life. Thus began a period of years of standing behind the counter wrestling with diapers (which were sloshing away in the washing machine in the back of the store), tending to the customers, keeping the books, ordering from catalogs, working with playlists, etc., that ended only after Rick was seven and Bob was nearly three and I was pregnant with David. It was then that we started construction on our house in the suburbs. That was in 1953.

Rick was a very bright little boy. While we lived in Berkeley, he was at the top of his class in the third grade. But when we moved out to Walnut Creek, he was behind the other children in the same grade. That was when I got a good picture of the differences between education in the inner city and outside of it. And Rick was already showing signs of confusion over his sexual orientation.

One day, Mel's mother cautioned me that I shouldn't allow Rick to do chores that were seen as feminine roles, like helping with the dishes. "He needs to work with his father more, on more masculine things," she told me. I'd already begun to notice that Rick was more likely to choose a feminine role in playing with other children, and Mel's mother's comment sealed those concerns. And after I read an article about children's sexual orientation problems in *Parents* magazine when Rick was about six, I found myself consulting his pediatrician about the issue.

The pediatrician assured me that this was an "idle fear," that parents in the United States were too concerned about such issues. She was from Europe, where—she assured me—gentle men were more readily embraced by society, adding that Rick was a *gentle* child who would not "choose" his orientation until sometime in adolescence.

Though I had no reason to doubt the pediatrician's expertise and her admonition not to worry, I continued to feel a general sense of foreboding about Rick's future, particularly as I witnessed Mel's increasing discomfort about Rick's femininity, expressed in an attitude of disapproval of his "ways." These feelings, I suspected, were fostered by Mel's parents. This proved to be a growing concern as we matured as a family.

I had asked the pediatrician whether others continuing to express their doubts about Rick's masculinity would influence those sexual choices during adolescence, when he began to explore his sexual confusion. I received no response from her at the time, but I knew that this was probably going to be a problem for Rick and decided that I would not be one of those influencers. I would allow him to gradually define himself in his own time and in his own way. Gradually and eventually, both Rick and I came to cope with the unexpressed reality of his sexual orientation issues, and the bond between us allowed a quiet acceptance on my part and space in which to grow on his part. The struggle for his gay identity caused him a good deal of grief in early life, during the unenlightened 1950s and 1960s, but allowed him to fully accept his complete sexual identity by his 21st birthday.

It was then that Rick invited me for dinner at the apartment in Berkeley where he had moved in with a wonderful young man named Ron. It was Rick's first meaningful gay relationship. He showed me the passport he had obtained for a trip he and Ron were taking to Europe, and he announced his gay status to me. Though I'd known and struggled with his homosexuality throughout his childhood and adolescence, it was the first time that we were able to openly speak about it.

It was this confidence in my ability to "read" my own children and to not be too impressed by those who had "read the book" and to override their advice that I gained in raising Rick that helped with the special challenges that were later to come with my youngest child, Dorian. It also helped with the two boys who came in between, Bobby and David.

IN 1950, WHEN RICK was five, I finally got pregnant with Bobby. I didn't believe it until I was about four months pregnant. I was slender, proportionate, but very small in stature. I had expected to show my pregnancy very quickly, but I remember walking down the street in downtown Oakland one day and catching sight of myself in a display window—I was wearing a green knit suit—and for the first time, I saw my body shape had changed and realized, for the first time, that this was pregnancy, because the doctor kept telling me I was pregnant but I didn't believe it because I hadn't yet seen it. But I could see now where, even though I was very small, I was curved where I had been straight and that that baby was here, inside! It was a thrilling experience to be pregnant. That was marvelous, even though it was not easy, because I had a five-year-old adopted child at the time. But it was a wonderful thing.

Then once it got started, when Bob was a year old, I was waiting to have the next one. I wanted to get pregnant again right away. Two and half years later, David was born.

I wanted another child. I wanted a girl. I became pregnant with Dorian when David was about four, and there was great delight when she was born. I didn't want to go back to Kaiser, where David had been born, because that had not been a good experience. But the young doctor who attended Dorian's birth turned out to be completely inept.

Dorian was born one month premature. I'd gone into labor prematurely after hemorrhaging severely. The placenta preceded the baby, not too common an occurrence, which probably contributed to our clearly inexperienced doctor's confusion.

Though the doctor met us at the hospital and was nervously standing beside the bed, Dorian and I never made it into the delivery room. She arrived unattended as her physician spent most of his time seeking assurances and assistance from the professionals around us.

It was not until Dorian was examined at six weeks that a pediatrician would discover that she was seriously anemic, and that she had suffered anoxia during delivery, a condition that results in the loss of brain cells from oxygen starvation during the process of birth. I didn't realize she was brain damaged until she was a year old. Our physician hadn't informed us of her state of being at birth. He in no way prepared us for what lay ahead.

But I gradually realized that she wasn't developing as the other kids had developed. That was not easy, because on the one hand, she was our first girl, and she was my only girl, and I had waited for and wanted her desperately. To have it dawn on me slowly that she had been born handicapped was really hard. This contributed heavily to the reason I fell apart when she was about two and a half or three.

4

INTO THE
LION'S DEN

IT'D BE GREAT TO say I was a feminist, but I didn't
know what that was.

Career was never anything to me. In fact, I never even attended
college. I never had a break between belonging to my father, whom
I respected, and belonging to my husband Mel, who was my best
friend, who I married after meeting him at the age of 13. It was a
predictable marriage. And I can't say that I questioned any of that.

I really, really was living a prescribed kind of life. Until we
moved to Walnut Creek and I found that I had to either choose
sides racially and politically or not survive emotionally.

We wanted to build a house, and could afford to when the war
ended. Mel's parents had moved to Danville, which was across the
eastern hills from Berkeley, and had a little truck farm and raised
horses out there. There weren't enough people in Danville then
to resist anything. By that time we had Rick and our son Bob,
and I was pregnant with David. And on the way to have the kids
ride the horses at Grandpa's house we would pass through an area
called Saranap, which was an unincorporated area between Walnut Creek and Lafayette, and Mel saw a vacant lot that he decided
he wanted. It was a little over a half acre, bordered by a creek.
There was no house on the property, but it had an old cement

swimming pool in the middle of it. And after spending years poring over magazines like *House and Garden*, *Sunset*, and *Architectural Digest*, we decided this was the spot where we wanted to build our home. This was in 1952.

But even though the property was in an unincorporated area, there was still no way we could buy it, because we weren't white. So we got a good friend, Dorothy Wilson, who was white, to make the purchase for us. She was the wife of Lionel Wilson, who later became the first black mayor of Oakland.

What I didn't know at the time was that with the end of the war, returning servicemen were using the low-interest mortgages available because of the GI bill to move into those communities east of the Berkeley hills, beginning the suburbs out there. And because the GI bill was administered locally rather than federally, the local banker could determine who could get mortgages in which communities so that white people would be coming to the suburbs, but black people could not follow due to strict racial restrictions. White people were trying to escape from people like *me*! We couldn't even get a bank loan to buy property above Grove Street in Berkeley, outside what was prescribed a black district. Even though we were a small enterprise doing business with the Bank of America in Berkeley, the bank wouldn't handle a loan for us. So we decided that if we were going to have to fight, we might as well fight for something we really wanted. So we went all the way to the suburbs of Diablo Valley on the other side of the hills.

So here we were, this young couple with two children and one on the way, moving into the midst of the lion's den. And we spent the next 5, 10 years in the awfulness of rejection, having to sort out where we were in that whole thing, becoming the objects of ridicule and hostility.

When the neighbors found out who had actually bought the property, it triggered a lot of anger. Sewall Smith, the Quaker architect who designed our home, was threatened, as were we. We got numerous threatening letters. One of them indicated the belief that Father Divine, who at the time was a great spiritual leader of the fundamentalist movement across the country, had purchased the property to put in what was called "a Heaven."[4] We got word that if we tried to stack lumber there to be used for building the house, some mysterious "they" would set fire to it.

They never followed through on those threats. It took six months to build the house, and sometimes I'd drive out there and just sit at the property watching the construction progress from my car. As time passed, local people would walk down, usually around sundown, to where I was sitting alone in my car on the roadside. They'd stop long enough to identify themselves and quietly, without fanfare, welcome me to the neighborhood. Over time, without letting their neighbors know that they had done so, almost every one of those families had performed that ritual. The local Improvement Association continued to take its stand against us being there, but individually, at least, some of the people in the community were not in tune with that, because almost everybody who came by said to me, "I hope that you will be happy here." It was a very strange kind of thing. What they could do collectively, none could support individually, at least not openly, not at first.

AROUND THAT TIME, ROBERT Condon, a well-known radical-liberal attorney, to use a description popular at the time, lived just around the bend of Las Trampas Creek, just over the bridge from our new home. He was a partner of Robert Treuhaft.[5] Condon and his wife, Eleanor, were both heavily involved in Democratic politics. When we first moved into the neighborhood, they offered to give a dinner party to introduce us to the neighbors because they were absolutely enchanted by our presence.

---

4   *EDITOR'S NOTE*: As part of his ministry, the Georgia-born African American minister Father Divine (whose original name was George Baker) established a series of well-known "Heavens," first in Harlem and then around the country, including one in Los Angeles, from the Depression years down through the 1950s. These were "residential hotels where [Father Divine's] teachings were practiced and where his [mostly black] followers could obtain food, shelter, and job opportunities, as well as spiritual and physical healing," according to *Encyclopaedia Britannica*.

5   At the time, I didn't know that Robert's wife, "Decca" Treuhaft, was the world-renowned writer and activist Jessica Mitford.

Our being the first people of color in the community gave them a chance to validate their liberal credentials. We were going to become their "cause." And I remember telling them absolutely not, they would not give a dinner party, because that would suggest that they were giving us permission to move into a house that we had built, and that we had a perfect right to own. And probably because of my speaking up, we never got to be friends with the liberal and colorful Condons. My refusal probably fell on their ears as an insult. I never really knew why their enthusiasm waned, but these were my suspicions.

But as we got pushed against the wall, what came out was a feisty, proud Betty in what apparently was the birth of this woman who later became a political activist. At that time, I was fighting for my right to be in that community, and, feeling perfectly deserving, wanted to set an example for my children. It was really, really personal. I was not a part of any movement. I was not a member of the NAACP or any other civil rights organization, or any political organization. And that was, I think, the beginning of my wanting to stand on my own. I remember telling the Condons, "I don't want you to feel responsible if I don't mow my lawn." I told them they couldn't give me permission to move into that community because that would also give them power to define my life as I lived it. I think that maybe those are the road signs that trace me back to a deliberate progression toward my political awareness now.

THE CONSTRUCTION PERIOD SPANNED from early spring to around November of that year. Rick had been transferred from second grade in a Berkeley elementary school, where he had been doing so well that there were suggestions from his teacher that we begin thinking about having him skip the next grade and enter fourth grade on probation in the fall. I knew that we would be moving to the Walnut Creek school system in late fall, so that had to be a consideration in just how the transition would be managed. But in the new school, Rick proved to be working at grade level. The differences in the educational levels between the inner-city and suburban schools surfaced immediately.

Mel and I decided that the least disruptive way to deal with the problem would be to register him at Parkmead Elementary in Walnut Creek for the fall semester while we were still living in Berkeley and have him ride out each morning with his dad while the house was being completed. Sensible solution, right? No. Disastrous, as it turned out.

This gentle eight-year-old was being dropped off each day into a hostile world of children who were expressing all of the venomous racism that was being freely expressed around their dinner tables each night, ugliness that the adults in their lives were not honest enough to show publicly to us, Rick's parents. It must have been horrendous. Poor little guy never mentioned it at the time, and I was too pregnant with David and preoccupied with toddler Bobby and the house building—choosing tiles, carpeting, bathroom and kitchen fixtures—to even be aware of his pain. It had all seemed so logical, sans the race element. After all, when we were growing up in East Oakland, the kids on our block had overcome their feelings of discomfort with us long before their parents did.

Sometime in the late fall I attended a parents' night at school and was asked by the principal just why I'd enrolled my child in this school when I didn't even live in the district. We'd moved into the new home that October, so the question held no relevance, but the principal's inability to meet my gaze suggested that his question was being asked due to pressure from other parents. Rick was the only black child in the school. We were only the second black family in the entire valley east of the Berkeley hills at that time. We were breaking new ground, reluctantly. We were developing growing defiance and a feeling of entitlement, but those feelings were not yet fully matured. There were still times when I wasn't all that sure that we were right . . .

Some time later, Marian Powelson, a sympathetic Jewish neighbor who had moved out to Walnut Creek from Berkeley after we did, mentioned that she'd picked up a flyer advertising a minstrel show fund-raiser that was going to be staged at the school.

Marian and I were both horrified at the thought, but didn't have a clue about how to deal with it. The image of white people in blackface, with kinky wigs and huge white-painted lips, was just too impossible to imagine in America of that day.

Just one day before the big show, I drove to the school with no idea of what to do, except that I knew I had to act. I walked into the principal's office and sat down to wait. He was off somewhere on the school grounds, but his costume was hanging loosely over the doorway. He was in the cast of the show, as were all members of the faculty. His costume was black and white and had bright red polka dots with baggy pants. I could feel my chest tighten.

He walked in, almost whipped around on his heels to leave at the sight of me, but turned back and continued into the room.

"This is wrong," I said quietly.

To his credit, he answered, "I guess you're right, but I didn't know that until I saw you there." He attempted an explanation. "Our faculty loves colored people," he said, "and we're only depicting them as the happy people that they are, with their songs and jokes—and stuff . . ."

My answer was, "Do I look happy?"

"No," says he, misery emanating from his eyes.

"Let's think this out together," says I. I explained to him that minstrel shows were originally conceived as ridicule of Negroes and were never a black thing. "We can't afford this kind of tradition to follow us through history, to continue to heap insult and degradation upon a people, least of all at the hands of educators, who, above all others, should know better," I told him.

"What would you have me do?" asks this man who by now was flush faced and clearly embarrassed beyond measure. I distinctly remember feeling sorry for him in that moment. It was clear that he was in a learning place, and that it hurt.

I told him that—with tonight's dress rehearsal at hand and the show only 24 hours away—I would not ask that they cancel. I did insist, however, that a portion of that night's rehearsal time be devoted to sharing my concerns, and I also served warning that the next evening I would be attending with my friend and neighbor Bessie Gilbert to see their show. And we did just that, front row center and unashamedly tearful throughout the entire awful performance.

It was a *dreadful* evening. Little was gained, I think. The experience was miserable for me. There was as much anger and resentment stirred by my action as there was enlightenment. I'm certain of that. It did little for my own kids, since I found it impossible to talk about most of these things. I was never sure that by doing so I wouldn't simply further alienate them from others.

Only a few weeks later, there was an Aunt Jemima pancake feed held by the local Chamber of Commerce at a downtown park.

WE'D COMPLETED CONSTRUCTION ON our new home on the banks of Las Trampas Creek in Walnut Creek. It had by this time been about three years since Mel and I had moved in with our three little boys, years before Dorian's birth, and Mel had returned to full-time managing of our record stores. Though I'd gained a few defenders, life was still strained and fraught with uneasy feelings of living under constant threat. I was left to spend my days pretty much alone, defending our right to exist in suburbia against the many stay-at-home wives who were now our small family's major oppressors. Their spouses, like mine, were away earning the mortgage payments in San Francisco and Oakland. In looking back, I realize it was a strange time for us all, a time remembered with pain and mixed feelings still.

Our status as the only black family in an otherwise white upscale community made us vulnerable to the hostility, but it also gave us visibility to those whose sense of morality would cause some to rise up to defend our right to be among them. This set the stage for a few weeks that I now see as the beginning of my adulthood and what would prove to be a gradual move toward full independence for me as a young parent with an emerging sense of self-worth. Over the years, I would be gradually convinced of my own power to stand alone. But up to that point, I had been sustained by my upbringing in the belief that a mere woman could not survive without the support of the men in her life. My proud father and very traditional young husband provided the power needed to survive the times, even if only in my head. I questioned not. Compliance, thy name was Betty.

Yet . . .

. . . for several days I'd been reading in the local newspaper about the growing hostility at a newly built working-class development in the town of Pleasant Hill, just a few miles away from our home in Walnut Creek. The stories involved a young black couple. He was a truck driver and his pregnant wife, a nurse's aide. They'd bought one of the modest homes and were being threatened by an angry Improvement Association that was distributing ugly pamphlets and posting signs imploring the community to come together to prevent them from occupying their home or brave the dire consequences. It was classic full-blown racist mayhem.

It was also not unlike the resistance that our family had experienced only a few years before. Our immediate neighbors had organized in the same way, threatening to burn our lumber as it was delivered. I'd rarely been confronted openly by my neighbors, however. They were far too outwardly well-mannered for that.

It had been a devastating period in our lives, but it had been lived through and we'd all learned from the lessons I would now share. It had also been a period when I was unable to speak for myself most of the time, but now I could speak on behalf of someone else and, in the process, finally have a chance to make *my* case, perhaps.

David Bortin, an attorney practicing in Walnut Creek and a member of a Unitarian fellowship consisting of some 25 young families, had read a letter I'd sent to the editor of the local paper after reading of the plight of the young Pleasant Hill couple. He'd called to say that he agreed with my position and offered to be of help. In the course of our conversation I mentioned that the Gregory Gardens Improvement Association had scheduled a meeting at the local school that very night and that I was thinking of attending. I'd go in order to let the community know that this change might be difficult, but that they would all survive in the end. Perhaps my experience could be of help.

David was concerned that I might be hurt and warned me to think about it carefully before doing such a thing. I convinced him that, while I'd learned how hurtful those angry and insulting words could be through hearsay, I'd never really *heard* the awful things my own neighbors had hurled in my direction, only those things that were rumored or written. I remember saying to him that "my color will protect me. That kind of viciousness is *never* expressed in the presence of colored people, only behind our backs. I will go and they will hear me out and then I will leave." Such innocence. David then told me that he would also be there and that there might be others. He would make a few calls.

That early evening I dressed carefully, drove out to the school, and parked in the crowded parking lot. I found my way into the auditorium and took an aisle seat about halfway up the center, attracting little notice from anyone.

The meeting was called to order by the president, who presented the problem and called quickly for testimony from those gathered. It was then that the rage began to fill the room. One after another they angrily expressed the reasons that their homes must be saved from the *"Invasion of the Undesirables!"* They spoke of threatened property values, etc. I felt like a spy among them. I grew increasingly uncomfortable. In my home community, only a few miles away, I had become the *blackest* of women, but here I was *invisible*. They'd failed to pick up on my "difference," my own "undesirability," so my imagined protection that they would not speak such words in front of a black person had failed because they didn't recognize me as a black woman at all. I was just an innocent witness to bitter racism for the first time in my life. I'd opened a new Pandora's box in my newly adopted role of defender rather than victim.

At the point when a woman viciously spat out "If we can't get the niggers out any other way, we can use the health department because of the filthy diseases they'll bring in!" I could be still no longer. I rose from my seat and walked to the front of the room, turned to face the angry crowd, and started to speak. I identified myself, then added, "I'm one of the *undesirables* you're speaking of."

I talked for about 10 minutes nonstop while the group stared in disbelief. The words threatened to dry up midthroat! I told them of our having built a home not too far away, about how that community had felt the same anger that they now did, about how we'd moved in under similar threats, and that I knew that members of my community who were resistant had every right under the Constitution to *feel* that resentment, but that that same Constitution guaranteed me and my family—as well as their new black neighbors moving into Gregory Gardens—the right to house our families as we wished.

Then, before a stunned audience, I walked straight down the aisle toward the main door leading out into the now menacingly dark parking lot. With a mouth bone dry and the panic about to take over my body, from behind I could hear chairs scraping against the floor of the auditorium and feet scuffling as people began to stir. I later learned that many left the meeting at that point. A reporter wrote in his piece the next day that it was clear that many were simply there out of a wish to understand the situation and to listen to their neighbors. According to his article, those attending were of mixed opinions and not acting as one. This was the last known meeting of the Improvement Association.

As I walked through the parking lot toward my car, I could hear quick footsteps rushing from behind in the dark and panicked! A stranger caught up with me just as I (by now in tears) frantically pressed the key into the door lock. He quickly assured me that he was with the press and that all he wanted was my name and phone number. "I need to get back in there to see what's happened in the wake of your speech," he said, "but I'll call you later." So saying, this friendly stranger disappeared into the night.

Then I felt a strong hand on my shoulder. It was not threatening. Immediately there followed a voice saying, "It's all right. I'm David." As promised, he was there to help.

By this time I was sobbing out all of the disappointment and disillusionment that unlikely scene had provided and the hideous rhetoric my family's presence in the community had unleashed.

David had been right. I'd foolishly underestimated the inherent danger of the situation, but his support at a time when it mattered beyond all reason also provided the hope that I so desperately needed in order to survive and grow into the power that would sustain me over a lifetime.

I found out later that after I walked out, a man had stood up before the people who were left and said that he knew me, and that I was one of the kind of people that were trained by the communists to do this kind of work. He had been one of my schoolmates from Castlemont years before, and I had thought he was my friend.

But that evening served as an introduction to the Mt. Diablo Unitarian Fellowship through David's acting on my behalf. (This small group later evolved into a formal church that is now known as the Mt. Diablo Unitarian Universalist Church.) Within a few short months I would become a member of the fellowship's board of trustees, beginning an active membership that would span the next 20 years and provide friendships that have survived the decades. A path would be set for adventures in social activism that would become the basis of my existence and the foundation of all that followed.

WITH SEVEN-YEAR-OLD RICK, toddler Bobby, and babe-in-arms David, I stopped at a little diner one afternoon just across Mt. Diablo Boulevard from the St. Mary's Catholic Church that we attended fairly regularly at the time. It was not a serious return to the faith of my childhood, but church was one of the few places in our lives where it was possible to be anonymous, and I hungered for that feeling.

Rick was involved in catechism classes in preparation for his first Holy Communion, and I'd just picked him up. It was around five o'clock and the diner was filled with noisy customers. I struggled in with the kids and chose a booth near the back of the place, near the restrooms. After a very long time, the waitress came over, I assumed to get our order, but, no, it was not to be. She announced with a grin, "You'll have to get out of here. We're closing."

The rest of the customers had gone silent. Some were also obviously enjoying my misery. It was the dinner hour. The place could not be closing. What was happening to us was obvious, but it was hard to know how to deal with it with my children looking on, especially Rick, who could surely understand. There was nothing to do but gather them up and—with hot tears scalding my cheeks—make my way back through the diner and to my car. I felt devastated! I was helpless to explain to my children what had just happened, but could feel their fear as they held tightly to my skirt and walked close to my body as we retreated awkwardly. With my arms filled with baby David, it was impossible to hold their hands and give them the reassurance that I would have had to pretend to feel. I felt the humiliation of being impotent to defend our right to be served in a public facility. These were first experiences for this little California girl having no history of experiencing the sting of such blatant bigotry. This was before the passage of the Civil Rights Act and the establishment of racially shared rest rooms and drinking fountains, but this was not Mississippi, but California. How could this be? This was my home over a lifetime, and that of my children.

Bessie Gilbert, my good Mormon friend—also new to the community—saw me pull into the driveway sobbing. She quickly dashed over from her house to be of comfort. "They were wrong," she told me after I explained what had happened, "but this is what life will be like if you don't get tough and deal with this sinfulness right now!" Bless Bessie. She sobbed right along with me at the unfairness of it all, but this good woman (she was much older than I and was a good six feet of solidly built "pioneer" woman from Utah) was ready to take on the world in support of the Reids from that day forward, and that she did.

I began to develop a thicker skin after a time, and a new sensibility that would protect us from such potentially painful incidents. My antenna picked up signals earlier, and by so doing lent more protection. Having Bessie and Al Gilbert ready to rescue me enabled me to develop a sense of stability and some confirmation of the rightness of our cause. Our families shared occasional meals. Their children, Jimmy and Evelyn, became the close first friends to our three over time. Being homemakers with absent husbands in common gave our friendship particular meaning. That deeply religious family served as a baseline against which to measure proper moral conduct. Without them, I'm not sure how I could have maintained any sense of my own worth, and I would surely have drowned in a sea of irrational hatred.

Because we had a swimming pool, which was not usual in our family, family members would come out to our home for picnics. And occasionally, as my kids grew up, cousins would come out, as well. But for the most part, while Mel was in Berkeley and Oakland every day and working in the world of music over there, I lost many of the connections I'd had for a time with my friends and family back over the hills.

In time the calluses began to grow on my psyche, and with the help of the Gilberts and a few others, a new kind of growth began to emerge and the responsibility to carry on seemed the logical way of survival. The rightness of my position was continually reinforced by my few new friends. In time the neighborhood began to relax and the young Reids as Threat to Humanity eventually subsided.

The Diablo Valley, while less than 15 miles from Berkeley and perhaps 30 miles from East Oakland, where I'd grown up and my family continued to live, was separated by what I thought of at the time as a row of hills covered by the "Eucalyptus Curtain" that protected white suburban Californians from the older, more racially diverse cities I'd grown up in. That's still true. Little has changed despite huge population growth and a continuing climb into upper economic status. The psychological distance eventually outran the physical distance, and in time it became impossible to exist on that bridge of connection. Years later it would become necessary to make the choice to not live a life of ambiguity. Conditional equality of that kind is far too costly to the soul, yet the riches garnered from having lived through the challenges can't be denied. I would not have missed a minute of it, and continue to draw upon those years as background in my work in the political arena in these tumultuous times.

WHEN FULL REALIZATION SET in that our only daughter and youngest child had suffered brain damage from birth trauma, it was devastating. Not only was I struggling with bringing up three little boys, I was doing it at a time that offered little in the way of help in the form of research into the field. The mentally retarded were still being hidden behind closed doors and were segregated from "normal" children in educational settings.

Not only that, but I had little exposure to other parents of children with mental disabilities and was left alone to try to "read" my special child for clues to the kind of parenting she would need in a world not designed to support or protect her. In the end, that was probably the wisest course I could have followed, because my "reading" of Dorian proved to be the most valuable asset as the years piled on. When it became obvious that she was functioning at the level of the retarded, she was somewhere between 12 and 18 months old. I'd depended upon the works of *The Child from One to Five* by Arnold Gesell and Frances L. Ilg, child psychologists whose work was the guiding force in the field at that time. I'd bought the complete five-volume set when we adopted Rick, before I felt competent as a parent (does one ever?). I remember telling Rick on his 13th birthday, "We'd better read this together, hon, 'cause if it's right we're going to hate each other by the time you reach 16!"

When Dorian was about five and I needed to enroll her in "the World," I visited the local elementary school to learn about what that scene would be like for my special child. When I walked into the portable classroom where such special-needs children spent their days, the classroom was quiet. They were brought to school each day by a special bus and spent their time separate and apart from other children.

There was a teacher seated on a low stool, holding up flash cards for several children who were attempting to parrot back the large printed numbers. There was a sadness that I was unaccustomed to. Dorian was much loved by her brothers and fared pretty well in social situations. As a family, none of us were scarred by the deficits she would carry for a lifetime. At home and in most social situations she seemed well accepted and psychologically

Into the Lion's Den

healthy. She developed early the capacity to stand her ground and knew how to get her needs met.

After spending about an hour quietly observing, I approached the teacher to ask if there was music in the classroom, and said that I'd be happy to volunteer to bring my guitar and sing with the children on a regular schedule. I told them that I'd learned by long interaction with my daughter that what I *said* to her might or might not be retained, but that what I *sang* to her was clearly integrated immediately and remained with her as a guide. However, there was no literature to back this up; it was one of the many techniques I discovered along the way. I'd made up songs that we shared that covered the rituals of our daily lives. I was told in no uncertain terms that the school district could not allow the *untrained* into the classroom with these fragile children. Nonsense!

I chose not to enter her into the public school system at all, but decided upon an alternative, a decision I've never regretted.

A group of adventuresome, idealistic teachers from the Mt. Diablo Unified School District had banded together and rented a small building in the nearby Alhambra Valley to start an experiment in education, Pinel School, patterned after Summerhill in the United Kingdom. They had opened with a summer program that three of my children—Bobby, David, and now possibly Dorian—could attend.

Pinel was based on the principle that children would learn what they needed to by being allowed full freedom to explore and grow with as little interference as possible, and to go as deeply into subjects as they wished with the full support of the faculty.

My only concern about Dorian's entering the program was how a child with a limited capacity for intellectual growth would fit into a program intended for children with the full mental capacity to take advantage of the freedom to grow. What about a child with a limited capacity for intellectual growth? I suspected that Dorian's main learning time in school would occur between her 12th and 13th birthdays, and at this point, I was mainly interested in having her socialized as we studied *how* she learned.

69

They were intrigued by the challenge and accepted Dorian as a student. We would all learn together. That decision paid off fully in the years that followed.

As it turned out, later psychological testing confirmed that Dorian had developed rote memory skills as compensation for the brain damage, and this, combined with the music that was so important in our household, made it possible for her at the tender age of eight to repeat back in proper sequence 22 items in the camping fireside game "I took a trip, and I took along . . . ."

Pinel worked for Dorian, and she thrived there until she was 13 and ready for St. Vincent's boarding school in Santa Barbara.

I learned to trust myself where her training was concerned, and over time my observations turned up some truths that have had lifelong implications. For instance: I learned that those who were the *givers* in life experienced growth and made out more successfully than those who were *takers*. This was a strategy that could be *taught* that might determine how she was viewed by the world. It's the reason that she later in life began crocheting miles and miles of "gifts"—scarves, afghans, bedspreads—presenting them to others, who are so visibly touched by her generosity that she gets immediate and life-affirming feedback. As an adult, she has created over 500 colorful afghans for wheelchair patients who reside in nursing homes. Whenever she's produced a couple of trash bags' full, we drive to an institution where she presents them (a dozen or so at a time) to appreciative patients, with the nursing staff beaming and cameras snapping. Dorian is a *Giver Supreme*.

THE CHILDREN ALL WENT to those public schools in Walnut Creek until they got to high school, and then I couldn't get anybody through high school. Rick failed. He simply stopped going. It got to be just excruciating in his last year, so he wound up getting his graduation picture taken and all that stuff, but he refused to graduate with his class.

Rick took it all. He didn't even bring it home, particularly. He absorbed it. And he was fighting being gay and being black in a white community. He was an adopted child who had been an only child in a home that biological children were later born into. He had so much pain to deal with throughout his childhood and adolescence. All these things were so difficult that I don't think he ever really got over being separate and apart. His misery was obvious and always a source of pain for me in watching him attempt to cope. I don't know how much of that I created for him in my effort to make a space for him in a hostile world, and when he died far too soon, it was very hard.

Rick's homosexuality was obvious from infancy, as I look back. When he was about six, as I mentioned earlier, I finally made an appointment with our pediatrician, a European native, to talk about what I suspected. She was shocked by my questions and let me know it. "This is simply a gentle child. You Americans are so strange. In Europe we allow our men to be gentle without suspecting homosexuality. In America it is different." She continued, "Children don't choose their sexual orientation until they reach puberty and it is impossible to tell anything until that choice is made."

I replied, "But if a child is continually having his/her gender questioned, isn't that choice somewhat prejudiced?" She didn't answer me. I figured that the information she had given me was suspect, and that my "gentle child" was gay, and that it was okay with me. One can't share life with a youngster for his five earliest years and not be smitten for life. My biggest problem would surely be to protect him from his "testosteronous" father!

I remember very athletic Mel—on the occasion of about the tenth time that Kenny, the neighborhood toughie, sent Rick home bloodied and bent—decided to teach Rick to defend himself. Perfectly ordinary thing for a dad to do, right? Wrong. I knew that this was a gentle child who would never make it against the strength of a bully like Kenny! This ritual went on for weeks. Mel would kneel with both hands held out before him for Rick to punch his little fists into. First left, then right, then crossover, then uppercut. It made me nervous to watch this futile game day after day.

Some time later Rick came home from play, nose bloodied, chin scratched, tears of humiliation and fear of facing his dad mixing with outrage! I ran to gather him up for comforting before

Mel could get to him, but it was too late. Mel popped out of the kitchen with "Why didn't you hit him like I taught you?" Poor little Rick: "But he wouldn't hold his hands up!"

There was no killer instinct in my child, and there never would be. He loved dolls and math, in that order. Built his first crystal set for radio reception when he was eight. Taught himself algebra with books from the library when he was in sixth grade because he needed it for a science project he was working on. This was a special child. He was bright, a linear thinker, sharp, and far more feminine than masculine in some important ways. And he'd been so since he came into my life at only a few days old.

WHEN RICK WAS IN third grade I attended a teacher-parent conference and was told that he was a good student but that he was often seen "passing notes with another little sissy boy." At about the same time, my mother-in-law visited the house and noticed Rick washing dishes. Her warning: "Betty, you mustn't let that boy do those kinds of things . . ." But the pediatrician had told me years before that boys needed to play with dolls and do household chores just as girls did because "they grow up to be parents just as girls do." An early feminist? At least she was partly right, but just a little twisted in her diagnosis.

The part that stuck was the part about there being a choice at puberty. I tried very hard to stay open and accepting so as not to influence that "choice," if there was the slightest possibility that the pediatrician was right. Never allowed myself to hint that I knew, at least until it was so obvious that Mel and I were unable to discuss his homosexuality at all. We never did, though I heard Mel call him a sissy in anger, but only once. He and Rick had a love/hate relationship that tore them both apart for years.

Poor Rick! His later alcoholism was his only out from the misery. He was, first of all, an adopted child in a family that later produced three more biological children. He was an only child until he was five, then came Bobby and, in quick succession, David. He suffered the agony of being the only black child in that suburban school where he was scorned. He was black and gay. He was a lost soul.

72

BOB WAS A HANDSOME child, also very bright and doing very well, except that he would not bend. Bob fought back, he fought back hard. That was okay with me as I grew into my own and, over time, learned to trust my decisions and judgments over those of others who thought his rebelliousness inappropriate. That attitude may have fostered a kind of recklessness on my part, an inappropriate faith in Bob's ability to determine his reality long before it may have been wise to trust him to do so.

David I took out of the public school altogether when he was in the third grade and put him in Pinel School. And when it was time for David to enter high school, after a false start at Del Valle in Walnut Creek, I sent him to live with a friend in Berkeley to finish school at Berkeley High School. By that time, I had given up on that suburban school system.

5

BREAKING DOWN, BREAKING UP

I GUESS DORIAN WAS two or three years old when I began my composing and singing. That came out of a mental breakdown, out of getting so needful that I came to the place where the internal artist trapped inside was able to emerge from me as a way of salvation. That part of me is only known by the people that I interacted with in the Mt. Diablo community. My Oakland/Berkeley urban world, the traditional, largely Creole world that I grew up in, never knew me as a writer/singer at all. And the people I came back to when I came back to Berkeley, the world of the University of California, the world of political activism that grew from my years as proprietor of Reid Records, didn't know me in my singing or composing life either.

But during those years in Walnut Creek, I performed concerts at a number of colleges. I was not quite admitting that I was doing this. I was Betty Reid who was willing to sing for you, but I didn't want to *be* a singer, just Betty who sang.

And composing was very private, very personal, a way of getting outside of myself to where I could gain the perspective to see the things that were happening inside of me. It was. I tucked all of that away after I came back into Berkeley in the early '70s.

WHILE ORGANIZING MY FILES recently, I discovered notes for an uncompleted song called "Meditation," which I composed while ironing in 1961, in one of those troubled days in our house in Walnut Creek.

The sun glows within me—the wind sings my song
the ebb and the flow of the tides mark my cycle of being
A Woman am I—and the day of my dawning is now!

I hold deep within me the buds of the flowr's of creation
their blooms . . . color all I behold!
with man I have moved throughout time
'roun this Garden of Being
A Woman am I—and the day of my dawning is now!

I've carried within me the kings, queens, and slaves of the ages
I've havened the dreams of the poets and painters and pages
I've borne, nurtured, buried the young ones
destroyed by man's rages
A Woman am I—and the day of my dawning is now!

The date on these notes places their origin long before the Women's Liberation Movement became an irresistible force for change. Prophetic?

I can only imagine very young Betty standing over that ironing board on a blazingly hot day, dreaming huge dreams of power and rebellion and starved for freedom from a life with no access to the depths of herself, trying terribly hard to fulfill the expectations of marriage and motherhood. Can't remember the time of day or what caused such a sense of determination and defiance. It must have been an epiphany that heralded a major life change. If I recall correctly, this preceded the beginnings of what would later be diagnosed as a period of psychosis. In looking back through a lens imbued with the wisdom of accumulated years, I know now that this was surely an unfortunate *mis*-diagnosis. It did not take into account the impossibility of being sane in a world gone mad.

I was a lonely young mother in a failing marriage with a troubled adolescent son struggling with his sexual orientation; with two little boys battling valiantly against racism in an all-white world of the suburbs, having to deal daily with rejection from an irrational, hostile community because of their skin color; and just beginning to come to terms with the growing certainty that my beautiful three-year-old daughter had been born brain damaged and would need a lifetime of constant care. I'm certain now that what was then seen as a mental breakdown was an *appropriate* response to an impossible set of life circumstances. The mind finds ways to protect itself from what it cannot process. Mine did it through art and music. What could have been more fitting?

I was able to move past that crisis and survive. I apparently used it well under the care of a sensitive and caring Jungian psychiatrist who, after months of reassembling my psyche, was able to broaden my understanding of what *normal* meant sufficiently to include myself with little alteration. No small feat, that. He gave me the strength to be *centered*, to stand pat, and to let the world adjust to *me*. I suppose that I'm still doing that, even as we speak.

Once full recognition of the bizarre reality in which I was living hit, my therapy was over and my *real* life began. *I* was not mad, the world was! The serious business of learning to live with and not deny my "madness" made survival possible, and does to this day.

I understand now that the strident lyrics of my song "Meditation" must have come near the point where I was still searching hungrily for strength from *outside* myself. I was still without a sense of having control of my own destiny. Still looking for my man to deliver *completion*. For all the brave words in this anthem of defiance, I was still a very lost young woman screaming for self-definition. I was forced to do that in the midst of also learning the hard lessons of racism and irrational societal rejection, all while trying to meet the challenges of motherhood. The convergence of traumatic events was devastating and had to be vented somehow.

Had I not found a way to express the pain, my personality might have splintered hopelessly. I had to find a way to travel great distances in such a way that my brain-damaged three-year-old could cling to my skirt and not become lost. The only *possible* escape was to move ever deeper into myself.

By virtue of hindsight, I'm beginning to see that the mental break may have marked the point where I came to terms with the fact that the source of all power is *internal. Where I stopped looking for completion from outside myself.* This may have been the place where I *grew up*, so to speak. The imaginative idealist and deeply knowing little girl of six reappeared (disguised as psychosis) and took over control, eventually. She'd survived into the 1960s—a childhood lived in a poor but proud black family during the uncertainty of the Great Depression, an adolescence supported by two or three imaginative and caring schoolteachers—and those few remnants of her were still there to save me when the persona that I'd so carefully created to cope gave way. *She* was the one with the magic and the ability to survive, I truly believe, and she still is.

It was at the age of seven that my First Communion training took over and all power was relegated to *"God!"* That is undoubtedly where the quiet acceptance of male dominance emerged and where I dared not ever even *think* that a lowly little girl could create *anything* of note. After all, *creating* was the province of *the Almighty*! The concept of divine intervention worked against my need to claim my own "edges," to *know* what *I* could or could not control, create, or define. I'd grown painfully into the ability to assume *personal responsibility* for my own life. I'd grown out of orthodoxy and into I knew not what, but *whatever* it was, it was mine. Maybe I was finally ready to accept the possibility that I was part of a random universe careening through space on the planet called Earth with no one at the helm. No small feat, that act of acceptance.

I wonder if it's really this simple? Could be. For all those reasons and more, I shut that little girl down early in life, though she surely remained in the subconscious and learned to *sing* Edna St. Vincent Millay's poetry in secret behind the garage at around age 11, and to read Maxwell Anderson and cry with Mariamne in

Winterset, and to pretend the world of Camelot into being when the real world became too painful. I probably shared all that as *sins* to Father Kelly in the confessional on some misguided Saturday afternoon before receiving Sunday morning Communion. What foolishness! How on earth is a child to know?

The fact is, I suffered a mental break that may have saved my life.

I'D EXPERIENCED SEVERAL EPISODES that were symptomatic of mental illness. It manifested in an inability to drive through tunnels or across bridges, even those not more than 100 feet long. I'd blacked out at the wheel of my car while driving through the long Broadway tunnel that separates Oakland/Berkeley from the Diablo Valley. Someone driving behind me saw me slowly slump behind the wheel. She straddled the double line to keep anyone from trying to pass while she followed me closely out of the tunnel. Fortunately, I was close to the eastern end, on the Orinda side, and with my car in gear but no pressure on the gas pedal, my car slowly rammed into the hillside at the exit. Woke up moments later with a highway patrolman at my window checking me out, with kindness.

At another time I attempted to drive across the San Francisco–Oakland Bay Bridge only to find myself unable to make it all the way across. I suffered a panic attack halfway and wound up mid-bay on Treasure Island. A Coast Guard escort eventually accompanied me to the other side—embarrassing, and equally dangerous. My tendency as always was to grit my teeth, crash up against my fears, and court disaster. I think that's called a suicide wish, but it certainly wasn't what I *thought* I was experiencing. Later in therapy I would discover that at least one obvious explanation was that both tunnels and bridges took one to definite destinations, and once entered into or upon, there was nothing to do but proceed through or over to the end. It was the divorce decision that I was simply unable to make. I'd been welded into my marriage by a promise made at the altar and from which there was no escape.

The mental illness sharpened my already overactive intuitiveness and sensitivity. I'd begun to write music and produce wildly colorful abstract paintings, all in an attempt at traveling without leaving home. Pure *survivalist* escape.

While that was all going on, I performed with other artists singing a growing repertoire of original songs from time to time, in concert or evenings among friends. One such evening there was a woman in the audience who turned out to be the wife of a film-maker studying for his master's degree at San Francisco State. She approached me at the close of the show with the words, "You're singing my husband's footage! If you'd be interested, I'm sure that he'd love to meet you. He's just about ready to add the musical score to his work. It's his master's thesis."

How exciting! Exciting enough for me to—in the days ahead—meet Charles Peterson and agree to make the trip to San Francisco State's studios to tape two songs for his documentary, phobias be damned!

The subject matter was of interest since it was based on the fact that the beacon light on the Farallon Islands in San Francisco Bay was to be deactivated soon, and when that happened, the wildlife would be in jeopardy. His documentary would be presented to the Coast Guard and to the Audubon Society in hope of keeping the light in operation as a deterrent to boaters approaching too close to shore. Any sea craft passing close to the island would cause some birds to leave their nests and take flight and, in so doing, their eggs or nestlings would be devoured by the less-shy gulls, who were fierce predators. An entire year's nestlings could be destroyed without casual passersby being aware of the peril they'd caused. An important message. This was enough reason to risk the drive across the bridge.

I'd learned from my therapist that what happened at such moments of panic was that my breathing would become increasingly shallow and I would eventually hyperventilate, losing consciousness at some point, as I had in the tunnel. And so I devised a way to handle such a situation. It was logical and sensible. I would drive across the bridge in heavy traffic with the windows open and singing all the way! When I sang, my breathing would be natural, determined by regular phrasing of the lyrics, and *even predictable*.

I could not run out of breath. It worked. On the appointed day I drove all the way from Walnut Creek, through the tunnel to Oakland, then across the Bay through another tunnel at Treasure Island and onto the busy freeway to South San Francisco.

There was an almost surreal occurrence at a film festival Mel and I once attended at Charles Peterson's to view his documentary, in which my singing was included. The second-place winner at that festival was a short film about the regularly crowded Bay Bridge at commuting hours. While the cars on the screen crawled across the bridge, the film's voiceover said, "On any given day, week, month, or year, motorists spend endless hours tied up in traffic. How is this time spent?" There came a scene of someone fixing a flat while cars piled up behind them, men in adjoining cars shouting at one another in fits of road rage, one of them shaking his fist at the other, and then, suddenly and unexpectedly, a woman in a yellow Comet gliding by, singing to herself in pure joy. Yes. 'Twas I.

I froze in my seat at the improbability of it. I remembered that day, when a station wagon had followed me so closely that I'd suddenly felt watched and rolled my window up to keep my space from being "invaded." Now it had not only been invaded, it also had been recorded for posterity, to be shown to anyone who wanted to see. I wondered if anyone around me recognized me as that woman, and how many things had to come together for me to both appear in those few frames of film and be present at a festival to observe those few frames in an obscure film I would otherwise probably never have gotten or taken the opportunity to see. What are the odds?

I never met the second-place filmmaker to share with him the miracle that we'd shared that night.

Charles Peterson's documentary, with my voice singing the score, went on to win prizes at the Atlanta Film Festival, in Toronto, and eventually in San Francisco that year. It was the film that was regularly shown at the Lawrence Hall of Science museum high in the Berkeley hills above the UC campus for some years. I discovered it there the day that I took my six-year-old granddaughter,

Kokee, to the museum, and as we walked down the hallway past the labs to the theater, the sounds of my own voice drifted out to us. I walked in with her just as the last song was being sung and the credits were running on the screen: "Music by Betty Reid." The theater was dark and empty. By this time I was remarried and living in Berkeley and far removed from my "poet" self. It was like listening to someone I barely knew.

MEANWHILE, MAYBE SEVERAL YEARS after the initial shock of our being out there in Walnut Creek, people who wanted to use me to authenticate their liberal views found me and I began to build this circle of liberals around me. And as the barriers did begin to come down, I gradually became socially active in the suburbs. I remember working with women on fashion shows at the country club. Mel and I enrolled as a couple in a class in social dancing at the high school and learned to dance in a big circle as white folks do. I remember giving luncheon speeches for church groups. I remember being advertised at the local Presbyterian church, a sandwich board out in front saying, "Betty Reid. Colored Housewife" to a group of wannabe-enlightened Presbyterians.

And I remember beginning my speech with that sign. I said, "You know, it seems to me that I could be described as an artist"—because at that time, I was doing a lot of painting and a lot of writing and music—"or I could be described as a mother, or I could be described as a political activist. But that sign limits who I am. I find it offensive." The women in the audience in that church cafeteria, with crepe paper streamers adorning the tables that held homemade casseroles and green gelatin salads, were stunned, but at the time I didn't have a feeling of being a part of anything, except the Unitarian church, which really, really was the change agent in my life.

THE PEOPLE AROUND ME didn't have the same questions I had about Catholicism. That became a real problem for me in my spiritual life, but I didn't have to confront it until I was a young married woman. I'd had to go back and accept the faith of our fathers because as far as my family was concerned, I was not married unless I was married in church. In order to do that, because I was marrying a non-Catholic, we had to go through—what was it?—three or four weeks of instruction in the fundamentals of the Catholic Church. And because Mel had previously had no religious affiliation at all, he was intrigued by the possibility of becoming a Catholic at the same time I had moved out of it. So that was a very rough period for me, because I was being married into a faith that I had outgrown. And I tried to subtly keep him from taking it too seriously. I kept him from being Catholic because I didn't honor it myself, without arguing about it, I just didn't *believe.*

But then when I was married for three years and had no children, I decided to adopt our first child. And that child came to us through Catholic Charities. Now, in order to adopt Rick, I had to agree to bring him up Catholic, because this was his biological mother's wish, and it had probably been a condition of hers for giving him up for adoption. So as a young adult now, I had to go back and retrace those steps of becoming a Catholic because I took my promise seriously. No matter where my thinking was, I was going to raise this child as a Catholic. It was a promise. So, then I had to go back and reexamine as an adult what I had walked away from and why.

I went to the priest in our parish in Berkeley and I told him of the promise, that I wanted him to help me to better understand my religion—and I was still saying "my" religion—because I hadn't taken on anything else. And after two meetings with him he said to me, "The problem with you, Mrs. Reid, is that you're trying to be—you're trying to be *intelligent* about a *faith* and the Catholic religion as a faith is a gift from God, and as such cannot be questioned." This was the end of the road for me.

And I thought as I walked out, "He doesn't know any more than I do." He was giving me a pat answer that I couldn't accept. And I never went back to him for further information.

But eventually Rick turned seven and I took him to register for First Communion at the local church, though I had not connected with the local church at all. But I was stubbornly determined to fulfill the promise I had made to his mother upon adoption. One day I would need to relate as much of his history to him as possible. That his mother had requested this condition was one way to let him know that she had cared about his future.

But when I went to pick him up after about the third catechism class, one of the nuns met with me and told me that I needed to have a talk with him about his understanding of the faith. They were going through the catechism lesson—"Who made the world?" "God made the world." I can go through that even now—and when she asked the question "Who made you?" Rick had raised his hand and said that his mother and dad had made him. She said that she couldn't accept that, but he couldn't accept anything else.

I couldn't support the church's position with him, but I kept trying. I sent him back. But this was a kid who was extremely bright in terms of science, he was way out there. He was building crystal sets when he was eight. He had tested in the 99th percentile in science and math. And he came in one day and said to me, "Mom, if it takes light so many years to get from this star to that star, how long does it take an angel to get there?" And I thought, *This kid's not going to make it—we're not going to make it—in the Catholic Church.* I walked away, and that was the end of it.

That's when I became a Unitarian.

I got introduced to a group of people—about 25 or 30 families—who were an offshoot of the First Unitarian Church of Berkeley and were meeting in a room in Walnut Creek. And I discovered that there was a religion, or at least a philosophy, that was not based on answers, that the answers are ever-changing. There were Christian Unitarians, there were Buddhist Unitarians, there were Jewish Unitarians, and there were atheist Unitarians—that was not where the emphasis was. The emphasis was on the questions.

So in order to satisfy my need for an intellectual community in which I could expand my religious beliefs, or at least my spirituality, and so I wouldn't have to answer my children's questions about why the sky was blue with "God made the sky blue and the grass green," I decided that this was the place for me to be. It provided a community that I could call home. And my children were raised in the Unitarian church, though one of them, David, is now a devout Catholic, and I go with him to church occasionally. Another of them, Bob, is probably an atheist, or at least an agnostic. And I feel successful in the spiritual guidance I managed to give them, because there's room for all of us, because we're not dependent upon answers, not even in the present.

IT WAS DURING THE period of time when I was trying to reconcile these different worlds—the black and the white—that I was moving between, and the different identities that were part of me, that I wrote the following song.

To Each of Me

To each of me, to love within the reach of me
and if this love could teach to me why each of me, in turn,
should torture so the soul of me, and tear apart the whole of me,
within life's play each role of me must speak to me, must learn
that blackness and the white of me are just the day and night of me
and not the wrong or right of me, can't you see, there's got to be
some answer to this planet's pain, my microcosmic world, insane,
if only I could make you see, it's here to see, just look at me
there is, within me, all of you from distant lands, the whole of you
the dreams, the heart, the soul of you, if you would only see
that black and white are part of it, my brown is at the heart of it
and blending was the start of it, and someday it shall be
that blackness and the white of us will be the day and night of us
and not the wrong or the right of us, the weak or might of us
then we'll be free.

MOTHERHOOD WAS DEEPLY FULFILLING. Being a wife was not. The seeds of discontent—years of feeling overworked and underloved—continued to erode my stability.

Little of what our daily lives were like was shared between Mel and me. He was working hard in Berkeley to support our new lifestyle—leaving very early in the mornings to make the rounds of suppliers and getting home exhausted near midnight, six days a week. We really lived different lives at that period. There were many years when that was so. We were very active parents, but he was only involved in the children's lives to the extent that he could be. We took them on family trips together when he took the time, for example. But our daily lives were not connected. The kids knew him as the guy who shaved in the morning in the bathroom. I mean, he was just not a part of our lives. He was not around to be the disciplinarian, so he was Santa Claus and the kids adored him. But there was very little companionship between the two of us.

Mel not only had founded a successful business that adequately supported the family, he'd also enjoyed the freedom and acclaim of being a professional athlete. That life offered travel and freedom from the responsibilities that fell to me. I was the stabilizer. He played quarterback for the Oakland Giants and the Honolulu Warriors, and also continued to play semi-pro baseball. There were other women who invaded our marriage from time to time, and that was hard, as well. All the while I managed our little business while raising our first and giving birth to and raising three more. I both wanted and needed to be out of the store to have the time to bring up the children, away from having to know about Mel's indiscretions. My parents were unsympathetic. "All men have some faults," says mother. "As long as he takes care of you, you shouldn't complain." That, and the fact that, as a Catholic, she added, there was no exit possible. "Adjusting and adapting to this harsh reality" was the only possibility open to me. Divorce was unheard of in my family, at least up to that time.

Besides, there was a kind of innocence about Mel. He was always contrite, and I'd become aware early in our marriage that this handsome Adonis was also functionally illiterate, a condition I would recognize much later as a severe case of dyslexia. He hid his problem well. Few knew. He'd compensated by becoming a fine athlete in both baseball and football, which took him as an All-Star through high school and Sacramento State College, and finally to the University of San Francisco. During his last semester at the University of San Francisco, I'd read and briefed him on his assignments. I was just out of high school at the time. He was a football major with a minor in history. He needed me, and I needed to be needed. In time we grew apart, painfully and with little recognition of how it all happened. In time, I was starved intellectually, but found that—since he was actually more comfortable with my family than I was much of the time—it was easy to see myself as the not-quite-normal one.

There is nothing more tragic than to find oneself at 40 living in a marriage with the quarterback chosen by an 18-year-old! At 40 Mel was still the quarterback, but he was now operating in a world that required an MBA, and that was eventually this good man's undoing. He surely did his best for us. He more than made up for his deficits by outworking everyone around him. All of the energy spent in being the best on the gridiron was applied to his business, and he accomplished miracles, despite all.

I must have been very difficult for him. I was pretty and bright, but a constant reminder of his failings. It took years to realize that being pretty was all that was required of me in this marriage. The rest—the bright part—was a liability.

I know now that I have never lacked intellect. I know that all the important things I ever learned, I probably knew when I was six. I suspect that I outthought my mother when I was about eight years old. But I didn't have the ego to support that until I began to enter later life and began to realize that the only difference between me and Mel was that I had a better sense of how much there was to be known, and he didn't. And that that was true of most of the adults in my life.

I suspect that I did little to support him over time as I lost myself in the world of the suburbs, where I was forced to struggle without his emotional support. Mother had been right. He did his best to provide well for his wife and children financially. But in time, it simply wasn't enough and we drifted apart. We eventually became strangers, both lost in space, without a clue to what was happening to us. My life in Walnut Creek had become more complex and less needful of Mel's presence. I eventually learned to survive without him.

But I almost didn't survive. It wasn't very long into the marriage when I began to realize that I had satisfied all the requisites of my parents and none of my own. Because there were things I couldn't talk about with Mel.

At that point, I was ready to move out of Walnut Creek and back across the hills. My marriage had pretty much ended, and I gave up the house and came to live in Berkeley and went to work at the University of California. I figured out that all the things that were bizarre about me were the things that were wonderful. I didn't need to be sane. All the sane people I knew were crazy. But that was at the base of all that, ending up with the dissolution of my marriage, the fact that I had not found this place where I could be whole and use all that I was. And I overcompensated. Fifteen minutes after I was divorced, I married a professor from the University of California. So that hunger certainly was there for something more.

THERE WEREN'T ANY MODELS for me. I could not have envisioned what my life became after my children grew up, how many of the societal issues I lived out. My first child, for instance, was gay. My last child is developmentally disabled. I had to care for my aging parents until they died, at 95 and 101, respectively. So all the issues of gay rights, of the developmentally disabled, of elder care—all of those things had to be lived out. And had to be lived out personally. I had to know what those things were. I think it sparked my life of activism, and very early. But not as a working woman. I worked in a dress shop in Walnut Creek at the time when I was anticipating, maybe, a divorce and needed to begin to explore how I would take care of myself.

People who came out of the South to work as sharecroppers—this is something that comes with my ranger self. I read treatises, doctoral papers, studies that are only now beginning to come out—people are only beginning now to study that era. But you read a sharecropper's experience, who, in Mississippi, would have to step off the sidewalk when a white person was approaching, and could be lynched for making eye contact with a white woman in a town. When you realize that those two people—that that white person who had the right of way on the sidewalk and that black person who had to step into the gutter to let that person pass—were then brought here to the greater Bay Area in huge numbers to build those ships, the black person with this huge expectation for a fuller life because those Pullman porters hadn't been lying, things were better in the West, and that white person, who was expecting a continuation of white privilege, came together into this cauldron of social reformation—I mean, forever—and that Mel and I, who had grown up without the complication of having to choose sides, who were first and foremost Americans, had to suffer the disappointment in that definition, as well as being lumped in with people whose experiences we had not shared, that had to be a period of huge, huge dislocation for us.

I can't imagine why it wouldn't have had its effect on who we became. Mel's life, in his business, became more centered in the African American community. My life became more centered in a changing suburban community. I was lucky enough to feel myself a part of that change. That's because I didn't compromise in my suburban existence, I brought my whole self with me into the suburbs and lived that out. And I think that we could not have stayed married. I think that we were destined to live separate lives because our lives took us in those directions. And I think it's telling that we remained friends after our divorce, that we reclaimed that 14-year-old-to-17-year-old-kid friendship, because we had parented four children. And that identity as parents withstood the divorce, even though I remarried—Mel never did. But even though I remarried, Mel and I remained friends until his death in 1987.

6

THE
MOVEMENT
YEARS

ONE EVENING IN THE summer of 2014, I crawled into bed early to watch the PBS show that had aired earlier in the week about that great event of 50 years before, "Freedom Summer." I'd waited until then since I knew it would be archived on the website and available through streaming. I'd felt no urgent need to view it before then since I knew that history so well that it would be simply a review of the past and little else; or so I thought.

At the end of the hour I was bunched up in a fetal position under the blankets sobbing until there was nothing left to feel. Over the years I'd screened out so much, I suppose for the protection of my own psyche. The rage that I'd been touting in my talks—which I'd thought I'd "outlived without losing my passion"—had only been suppressed, and it burst through the walls of protection so carefully built over those decades that I'd convinced myself the storm was over. Not so. The explosion of reawakened feelings of utter fury and fear left me limp and unable to sleep until nearly dawn.

Those powerful feelings had enabled me to come through the '60s civil rights revolution relatively unscathed, though I did suffer a mental break at one point. The rage and fury and fear now exploded back to life again. I'd clearly forgotten the duplicitous role played by Lyndon Johnson in the attempted seating of the Mississippi Freedom Democratic Party as delegates at the 1964 Democratic National Convention, the sheer eloquence of the MFDP's Fanny Lou Hamer in describing the suppression of black would-be voters in the state. . . . All I'd remembered until watching the PBS footage was that Johnson had ushered in the 1965 Voting Rights Act and the War on Poverty.

I continue to believe that it was the seeds of social change sown in the Bay Area during the Home Front period of WWII that gave form and substance to the civil rights revolution of the '60s, and that those influences continue to radiate out from here into the rest of the country and the world to this day. I suspect that it may well have been those of us whose lives spanned both those eras who shaped what was then the future.

THEY HELD WHAT THEY called the Walnut Festival every fall in Walnut Creek, with a parade through the downtown section. I took the children with me every year. The festival and parade in 1963 took place not long after the bombing of the 16th Street Baptist Church in Birmingham and the killing of those four little black girls.

Our church entered a car in the parade with handmade signs covering the sides reading "Our community cares" to bring the community's attention to the Birmingham church bombing. George Fujioka, Japanese American, a member of our church, was the driver, with Dr. Howard Diller sitting beside him in the front seat. We'd self-selected deliberately to show the diversity of our church community. I was seated at the rear atop the folded canvas top of the convertible, with Dorian and a few children of church members in the back seat. I was dressed totally in black with a black veil draped over my head, covering my face, a woman in full mourning.

We brought the car to the staging area at the high school football field where all the cars and floats were being organized in preparation to enter the line of the parade. Two or three hours we sat, uncomplaining, before they would allow our convertible in. Cars that had come later were put in ahead of us by the marshals, and they kept putting us back and putting us back. When they finally allowed us in, they made sure there was almost a block between our car and the units ahead and behind us, so it didn't look like we were officially a part of the parade.

As we finally entered the parade and were moving slowly down the street, it was very quiet except for an occasional hiss from the onlookers. I remembered thinking about the young children in the car with me and knowing that they couldn't possibly understand what was happening. Some people waved, but they were largely people whom I already knew. Testing the mettle of that community, which I found myself doing every now and then, as often as not disappointed me. I had thought we were making progress when we really weren't at all.

I think my activism at this point was an embarrassment to Rick, maybe, because he wanted everything to be quiet. Whether this was less a case of racial sensitivity than just a case of teenage angst, I didn't know. It might have been either.

I WAS ALREADY IN therapy that November of 1963 when JFK was killed. I was at home and I think I had a therapy session at twelve o'clock. And my sister Marge was dying. My sister died and Kennedy died within hours of each other. Beautiful Marjorie died after a long unidentified illness on the morning of the day that President Kennedy was assassinated. So in that period, it all sort of runs together, because within hours, I was on the train with my kids heading for Los Angeles to bury my sister. And the entire train was in mourning for a dead young president, so it was all of one piece for me.

Those two deaths are so blended in my mind that I had a hard time separating them out. In fact, I don't think I ever really was allowed to grieve for Marjorie, because everything was in grief mode, everything, the whole country and the world. Marjorie's death got lost in it.

We had been separated for many years. I didn't know her very well after she moved to Los Angeles. She lived in Kansas City for several years before moving to Southern California. So we weren't particularly close, but I felt her loss. It saddens me, still. I've never felt that she was properly mourned. Maybe I'll find a way to do that one day.

WHEN THE '60S BEGAN and the Civil Rights Movement started in earnest, I was still living out there in the suburbs, not quite black enough for the city and not quite white enough for the suburbs. I was still living with Mel, but he and I were drifting toward separation and divorce. And the Unitarians were my community.

The Unitarians in the Diablo Valley area were very effective people, and this was where I was able to test my mettle against a lot of things. They supported me in my growth toward blackness. When the national Black Unitarian Universalist Caucus formed in the Unitarian Church, for example, I wasn't sure whether it was a step forward or a step back, because we'd worked toward integration for so long. But our minister, Reverend Aron Gilmartin, who was white, had attended the annual conference in New York where many of the black delegates walked out and formed the first black caucus in this most liberal denomination.

Upon his return from the East Coast, Aron was obviously moved by what had happened, and immediately sought me out to convince me that this was something I needed to know about, there was something new going on in the denomination, and it was important. It was plowing new ground politically, and was something that we had to go through together.

The church fully supported me in exploring the black movement nationally. They sent me to Chicago to the first National Conference of Black Unitarian Universalists. It also followed that Aron Gilmartin entered the race for the presidency of the

Unitarian-Universalist Association that year, using his power to join with the emerging black voices of the denomination.

I attended three Black Caucus meetings, one in Chicago, one in Detroit, and the final one in Cleveland. That's where I met Jesse Jackson, who was then heading Operation PUSH (People United to Serve Humanity) out of Chicago. Jackson was a speaker at the Chicago caucus at the Hotel Windermere. His fiery rhetoric was exciting and stirring. His words moved me ever deeper into the Movement. Henry Hampton was one of the leaders of the group. He was the producer of the brilliant PBS documentary *Eyes on the Prize*. Among the many black intellectuals I met at that Chicago Black Caucus were various poets, writers, and political leaders, such people as Carl Stokes, who would later become mayor of Cleveland, and Lerone Bennett, author of *Before the Mayflower*. Bennett was associated with *Ebony* magazine at the time. There were artists who would, over the months and years ahead, become nationally recognized leaders of the Black Power Movement. Black leadership up to that time had traditionally come from the fundamentalist black church, and these people I met were the new secular intellectuals of the Movement. It was life-changing to find myself among them for the first time.

ATTENDING THAT FIRST Black Unitarian Universalist Caucus conference in 1968 would be my first experience with what I later came to understand was my political black birth.

I had arrived in Chicago somewhat resistant to the Black Movement, but I found myself so excited by what I found there. I was seated next to Mrs. Countee Cullen, the writer's widow, in a room full of black intellectuals from all over the country. I came back feeling so high from that experience that on the plane coming home, I wrote something called "Ebony the Night." It was the experience of blackness as a positive force for the first time.

As I lie 'neath the stars on this night of my day,
playing the game that some poets play,

find synonyms for black both poetic and good.
Sounds simple? You try. I do wish you would.

The world made the rules and established the ante.
Proclaimed white as sinless and black straight from Dante.

Ebony the night, ebony satin bright.
Star jewels held in black velvet hands of ebony the night.

Onyx, set with a dream that weaves through my mind 'til I seem
black born and kiss warm, black jet jazz of love, onyx the dream.

Black image cries behind shuttered eyes
trying so hard to be good.
Glaciers and skies of ebony lies, I'd sing them away if I could.

Ebony the night, cradle me, the night.
Black chin cupped closed in black velvet hands
of ebony the night.
Ebony, ebony the night.

IT WAS DIRECTLY out of my association with the Unitarian church that my work with the Black Panther Party began. This was sometime after one of the Panther founders, Huey Newton, was jailed, accused of killing an Oakland police officer, and the Panthers were demonstrating down at the Alameda County courthouse in Oakland demanding his release. I would drive in from Walnut Creek to march with them. That's the way I met Kathleen and Eldridge Cleaver. And afterward, Aron Gilmartin and I would collect money in the suburbs around Diablo Valley for the

Panthers, produce small fund-raisers to benefit their work, and then he'd drive us to San Francisco in his little green Volkswagen to drop off the checks at the Cleavers' apartment.

IT WAS AN AWFUL time when Dr. Martin Luther King, Jr., was assassinated. I think I felt more hopeless when he was killed than when Kennedy died, because by that time, I was firmly, firmly black-identified and had been active politically throughout that whole period. And his loss—I felt that it was the prelude to the kind of anger that I expected but also intensely feared.

When Malcolm X was still alive, I had begun to see him and Martin Luther King pretty much as one in that because of what I knew of white racism, because I had lived so much of it leading up to that period. I was under the impression that Malcolm X was making possible the work of Martin Luther King.

Even though they appeared to be on two very separate paths, I felt they really weren't that at all, that the threat of a Malcolm X was making possible the kind of nonviolence that Martin Luther King was preaching. And that King's work would not have been nearly as successful as it was and he would not have appealed as across race lines to the extent that he did without the threat of Malcolm X hovering menacingly in the background. I suspected that both leaders knew this and were taking advantage of it, unstated, as a strategy.

CREATING AND PERFORMING ORIGINAL songs became my way of processing and making sense of the terrifying history that we were living through at that time. One of them from the Movement years was called "Sign My Name to Freedom." It was based on letters 18-year-old university student Susan Sanford wrote home to her family from her work with the Civil Rights Movement in the Deep South, and which her family shared with me.

Among my white friends at the time was Susan's father, Don Sanford, who had raised his two daughters for many years in a politically liberal environment after the death of his wife. I believe

I may have had Susan, his eldest, as a student in my religious education class at the Mt. Diablo Unitarian church.

In the Freedom Summer of 1964, Susan was ready to try her wings with the Student Nonviolent Coordinating Committee as a volunteer teacher in a Freedom School in Canton, Mississippi. Along with others, she was giving up her university education for a while in order to become a part of the struggle for civil and human rights, the challenge of her generation.

There was no possibility of my joining that struggle since I had four young children needing care. This struggle was far beyond my reach.

The evening before Susan was to leave for the hostile Deep South, I was invited by Don to join the family for a farewell dinner. This was happening at a moment in my own history when my marriage was slowly disintegrating. I had a little necklace of pearls that had been a gift from my young husband, Mel, on our wedding day. I decided on the night before Susan's departure to give the pearls to her with the words, "I'd love for you to wear this under your T-shirts as you work, to keep you safe, and to give me a presence in this important undertaking."

While Susan was at her dangerous and important work in Mississippi, I wrote "Sign My Name to Freedom" about how I imagined she was facing her fears and the great challenges of her days. It was during a period when 37 black churches in Mississippi were destroyed by arson.

Monday mornin' . . . streets are bare . . .
seems as how dey don' want me nowhere
since ah went to the Courthouse and sign mah name to freedom.

daughta say, "mustn't run . . .
sound the trumpets . . . the Kingdom's come!
Mamma go to the Courthouse
'n sign yo' name for Freedom."

Fields afire—cotton flamin'
'neath the summa skies
Shrouds 'o White . . . no name namin'.
Dey don' know 'dis dream cain't die

Churches burned—deacon dead
still ah know it's like daughta said
ain't no turnin' back now—
Got to sign mah name to freedom.

Young folks heah a'roun' mah table talkin' through the night
faces heah ah cain't label—
brown ones blendin' wid da white . . .

Sunday mornin' . . . church ain't there
bombed it Wednesday but ah cain't care

God was down at the Courthouse day
ah sign mah name to freedom

Ma Lawd was down at the Courthouse—day ah sign mah name.

At the end of summer Sue returned home, having completed her work successfully, and the pearls were returned to me.

MY MENTOR DURING MY early activist years of the '60s was my Unitarian minister, Aron Gilmartin. I can figure out that he was an active Socialist. He must've been. For example, he introduced me to one of his best friends, a houseguest visiting from the East Coast, Norman Cousins, a onetime Socialist candidate for president of the United States. People have told me that I'm a Marxist. I have never understood even what a Marxist is, except that whatever it is, Gil has claims on my conversion. He was an uncompromising liberal progressive. And I don't know whether I learned from him, in words or by inference, that a belief was not valid unless acted upon, that this is how one activates a belief, and no other way.

That led me into a series of political acts that involved standing with others on the roadway to Port Chicago in a protest, twice. The first time, I flunked.

The American Friends Service Committee, Quakers, had been out on the road to Port Chicago at the Concord Weapons Station trying to stop the munitions trucks that were going in to be unloaded. So I drove out there and stood on the side of the road. And for the first time, I realized that I could protest a war. This was during the early days of the Vietnam War.

There weren't any more than 10 or 12 of us standing in protest. Most were people I didn't know. As we attempted to stand our ground, cars were driving by filled with families. More often than one might imagine, the adults in the cars would hold up their middle fingers to us and scream out obscenities as they passed. I remember wondering how people could do that with children witnessing it. And the feeling that I was *causing* those people to do such despicable acts, somehow just because I was standing there, that's the first time I can remember feeling thoroughly confused. Uncertain. Conflicted.

And finally the trucks came by. They would travel as close as they could to us without striking us. Those people that I was standing with would not give an inch, but I was falling back each time. And I can remember the trauma even now of not knowing what a war was like, of realizing I'd never been in a war. That I didn't know what war was, not really. But I knew what a truck was, and I was afraid of those trucks.

Finally, I picked up my skirts and I ran and climbed into my car. I was in tears. I drove home feeling thoroughly disgraced, because I had been great, theoretically, around war, but I was terrified of trucks and I wasn't able to do what I had wanted to do. I remember driving straight to the church to explain to Gil that I had failed miserably, that I couldn't live up to my expectations for myself. He said, "Only for the moment, Betty. You will go back." He told me that we can only do what we are able to do at any given time and under a single set of circumstances, and we must not feel unsuccessful in any one attempt. The opportunity will rise again to do something else, and the courage to act will rise with it.

And I did go back. And I was able, some years later, to go back to Port Chicago and demonstrate with Brian Wilson, who later had his legs run over and lost them in another demonstration at the port, one I didn't attend. But that's when I became a real activist, during those years, because I learned in Walnut Creek that there was no such thing as a middle-class black except in the mind of a middle-class black. We were still in nigger status, and that would hold for some years before we would blend into the whole, if ever.

THE WAR IN VIETNAM had reached a peak, and with it demonstrations against it. That was especially true in the Bay Area, which was a port of embarkation both for munitions for the war and for young men inducted into the service.

I joined in.

After one of those demonstrations in the early '70s, I sent a letter to my friend Robin King, a deejay at a local radio station, about the events of that day.

"I'm extremely tired tonight," I wrote.

> I guess the old term is "soul weary." Bob, my 17-year-old, is caught up in the dilemma of the draft. He was among the demonstrators [at the Oakland Army Induction Center] on Monday and again on Wednesday. As he told his dean upon returning to school on Tuesday (after having cut classes), 'I'm facing the draft in another six months. There are lots of things that I need to learn in order to make my decision about that—maybe the decision of my life. There's nothing here in school to help me to do that, my answers were out there in the streets. I had to go.' The dean (rather untypically, I thought) was very understanding and admitted that, were he in Bob's place, he would surely have done the same. No disciplinary action.

On Wednesday, I joined the demonstrators. It was interesting and frightening. You know that courage in battle is not one of my strong points, and, for all the words we use to justify actions once taken (when they're controversial), when the evidence is in, I was really there taking my risks in support of Bob [not knowing until later that he was there himself].

[In the middle of the demonstration, a] crowd began to run around the corner to the other side of the induction center. I joined them, and, as we rounded the corner, I could see the police marching in formation behind a paddy wagon moving toward the side entrance. The protesters formed a marching picket line. Together we marched and sang and yelled and prayed while the police gathered up those who were blocking the doorway.

In all, I was there for about three hours, singing "We Shall Not Be Moved," sharing in the bravery (which it was possible to "catch," even for a soul as timid as I), and witnessed the arrests of ordinary people, valiant youngsters. Saw clerical collars, nuns in their habits and wimples, and academic stoles. There was a contingent of youngsters from Berkeley High School, complete with banners and accompanied by a young Episcopal priest, sitting in at one of the entrances. Saw a young man cry as he loudly pleaded with a busload of inductees not to go! I yelled, "Hell no, don't go!" along with the rest and I meant it way down in my soul.

Looked into the faces of the Oakland Police Department. Now that is an experience. I know that these men are someone's next door neighbor—that they put up Christmas trees, love their mothers—but they seemed completely dehumanized. I had the wild feeling that these men were so conditioned that one could almost imagine some giant wizard at a master switch down in the bowels of that garage, an activating switch of some kind . . .

A Pioneering Life

At home in 1994.

Lottie Allen Charbonnet, my mother. This was taken in her 90th year.

My father, Dorson Louis Charbonnet, as a young man—26, I believe, but that's a guess. He was one of seven brothers and four sisters, though I've learned recently that his mother, Victoria Morales Charbonnet, bore 17 children. I know only of those who survived childhood.

My maternal grandfather, George Allen, Jr. (though I don't recall anyone ever referring to the "junior," a much later designation, I think).

The eminent Louis Charbonnet, my paternal grandfather, who was a noted figure in New Orleans. His obituary spells out his record of achievements and is available online.

St. John de Bertrand's Convent of the Holy Family Sisters in New Orleans was built by my grandfather, Louis Charbonnet, assisted by my father and his brothers. This was the first Order of African American nuns established in the country. It still stands out on Gentilly, near Dillard University, but is no longer a convent, I'm told.

Family photo taken shortly after our arrival in Oakland in 1927. That was the year of the great flood. In the back is my mother's brother Herman Allen. In the next row, from left, are my mother, Lottie Allen Charbonnet, being embraced by Sarah LeBeouf; Louise Breaux Allen, Papa George Allen's third wife; and Isabel, Papa George's sister. In the front row, from left, are my youngest sister, Lottie Charbonnet, at about 18 months, being held by a friend of Aunt Louise's named Teen-Dah; my older sister, Marjorie Charbonnet; me (Betty), and Audrey Kingsbury Allen, the first wife of my mother's brother Frederick Allen.

Betty Charbonnet, graduation photo from Castlemont High School, Oakland, 1938.

Three Charbonnet sisters—the youngest, Lottie Emelda; me; and Marjorie Mae. I'd guess this was taken around 1945. I'm the lone survivor of the three.

Photo taken in 1927 just after our family's arrival in Oakland. Papa George is the man standing at the back. I am the child seated in front.

Staff of Boilermakers Auxiliary-36 in Richmond, California, a segregated offshoot of the Labor Union into which all black workers were placed. I'm in the front row, far left. My sister Marjorie is standing in the back row, far right.

April 1942. I was at a florist choosing the flowers for my wedding in May.

STATE CHAMPS

Baseball was a popular American pastime in the early 20th century. Minor league games drew big crowds up and down the coast. Berkeley's California Eagles were the first African-American team to win the state semi-pro championship (in 1940).

Mel is pictured here standing in the middle of the back row, 1940.

Mel's father, Thomas Reid, working the loading dock at Wonder Bread in Berkeley.

My marriage to Melvin Adelbert Reid on May 24, 1942, in the garden of the home where I grew up on 83rd Avenue in Oakland.

The year is 1953 and we've just moved into our new home in Walnut Creek. Rick is standing at the left, with Bob in my lap and David in the womb waiting . . . Mel is standing behind us

The year is 1953 and we've just moved into our new home in Walnut Creek. Rick is standing at the left, with Bob in my lap and David in the womb waiting . . . Mel is standing behind us.

The christening of Dorian in 1957, where Rick, her oldest brother, is named her godfather. Pictured left to right: Rick, Mel, Bobby, David, and me holding Dorian, at the Pine Street Unitarian-Universalist temporary chapel.

Taken for a magazine cover, circa 1950. I believe the setting is at Lake Merritt Park in Oakland.

Taken by the local newspaper at the Annual Convention of Unitarian-Universalists held in Cleveland, Ohio. I was performing as a member of the Black Caucus of the denomination. The year is probably 1967 or 1968.

At the Asilomar Conference at Stebbins Institute in the mid-'60s. We attended this yearly for about 15 years as a family. Friendships from that period have maintained over the years through our children, now grown.

Behind the counter at Reid's Records. This photo was taken for an article written by columnist Lee Hildebrand for the *East Bay Express* in the late '60s, I'd guess. I was then fully engaged in reestablishing Reid's Records and overseeing the reclamation and construction of 49 units of low-income housing across the street from our shop. It was the completion of that project that brought me to the attention of the state of California, which named me a Woman of the Year in 1996, so I'm guessing that the year here is 1995 or early 1996.

Recent ad for Reid's Record Store in Berkeley.

Arriving at the 1972 Democratic National Convention in Miami Beach, Florida.

Arriving at the 1972 Democratic National Convention in Miami Beach, Florida.

At the Democratic National Convention in Miami Beach. I'm a McGovern delegate in the California delegation led by Speaker Willie Brown.

Bill Soskin and me on our wedding day in 1973, at our home on Grizzly Peak Boulevard, high atop the crest of the Berkeley Hills.

At home in Berkeley, 1973.

Wedding day, 1973: my second marriage, to Dr. William F. Soskin, at a ceremony held in our home. There were no guests present, only Rev. Aron Gilmartin, who officiated, his wife, Eve; and our best man, Dr. Leonard Duhl.

I sang at my own wedding.

Woman of the Year poses with California
Assemblyman Tom Bates, 1996, in Sacramento.

That wondrous evening in 2015 at the tree-lighting ceremony with the Obama family in Washington, D.C. I'd been sent by the Department of Interior to introduce the president on national television—a PBS special—and to meet the First Family.

This photo was taken for an exhibit for the Anza Trail project at the John Muir National Historic Site in Martinez, California. The Anza Trail commemorates an expedition in 1775–76 in which Spanish Lt. Colonel Juan Bautista de Anza led more than 240 men, women, and children on an overland journey of 1,200 miles to settle northern California. The Anza party was made up of multiracial adventurers, a group in which someone like me might well have been a member. In that context, I felt strangely at home in my universality, rather than my more limited African American identity.

This was taken on my 91st birthday at the Visitor Education Center at the Rosie the Riveter/WWII Homefront National Historical Park. That trip up in the cherry picker was a gift from staff, something I'd coveted all year!

At the Visitor Education Center, circa 2015.

On the way home I suddenly felt my blood run cold. It dawned on me that this was the way it would be with my lovely gentle poet Bobby. That here was the missing piece, so obvious as to get lost in the hysteria of war. Because I am so awed by the Vietnam scholars, the great debaters, the arguments pro and con, to "escalate," to "de-escalate," to "withdraw," "extend the bombing," "the infiltration of commies within the ranks of the peaceniks," all irrelevant.

Speaking for me, I'm here to stop the "Soldier Factory." These [soldiers] were all "Bobs" unable to see themselves in the role of killer. It's the same as the "Cop Factory." These are loving fathers and husbands, good neighbors. Conditioning of the sort that must be experienced in order to produce those inhuman creatures must be stopped.

I now know why I will go back. Yes, even tomorrow, when violence is expected. Scared? Yes. Paralyzed? No. My Bob is another Johnny—musket, carbine, M-1—what's the difference. After a trip to the Soldier Factory, he will accept just as millions before him have, down through all of time, that this is right in order to save the world.

I'm an ordinary middle-aged wife and mother. I've seen for myself. I've no more doubts. Anyone with an ounce of integrity left must act, and now, if any of us is to be saved.

Why this letter? Tonight as I was driving home from one of my endless trips to deliver kids, I happened to tune in to [your radio station]. You were just beginning to read from a piece by Henry David Thoreau. I parked beside the road and listened to its conclusion. Felt so moved. Wondered if you knew how those of us who have been on the line have needed just that? I felt soothed. Bathed in the silence of the night for a while. Started the car up again and came home to write this note. Our friendship has known many fine moments, friend, but tonight was a special time. The more meaningful because I could take this familiar voice as a personal message, just to me, but at the same time to know that there are others out there who, like me, will be comforted by the love and conviction in your voice. It was one of your finest hours.

I do so love you, friend,

Betty

7

AN
EMANCIPATED
WOMAN

AT DINNER A COUPLE of days after Christmas one year, my son Bob was trying to think back on just when he believed I started life as an emancipated woman. "It was after the death of my grandfather and my father—the main men in your life—that I think you found your voice," he said.

I wholeheartedly agreed at the time. I think that for most of my life, I believed that I came into my own only after being forced to confront life without the men in my life who defined me. I think that I saw them as the positive space to my negative, that I had always been the other half of a whole. But in retrospect, this was clearly not so.

I believe now that I made the first real step toward independence during the traumatic meeting at Gregory Gardens, when I stood up to confront the biased activists of that community on their own ground. I had suddenly stepped out of the role of *victim* and taken on that of *defender*. It was on that night in that frightening meeting that I tossed off the shroud of victimization that had held me in its grasp and became a full-fledged mature *woman*. I had finally broken free.

Looking back now, it's clear that it was not possible for me to negotiate a way for that mature woman to exist in a marriage entered into by a 20-year-old girl with no expectations of emancipation and no idea of how to live in freedom. I was suddenly on a collision course with a reality that life had not prepared me for.

It must have been the Gregory Gardens event that changed the course of my life and started the slow erosion of my first marriage. I'm wondering now why I didn't see that the path I'd taken that fateful night would inevitably lead to full independence and complete emancipation at some point.

I can't recall ever speaking with Mel of my trip to Gregory Gardens. About that time, so much of my life became secret and unshared, and that probably caused the mental break a few years later, when my distinctly different realities could no longer be held separate, and when no amount of logic could bring them together with any semblance of order.

It was during those years that the threat to my sanity became real and the artist Betty came into being. She was my defense against the growing split that would eventually have to be tended to.

The secret "Betty" that friends and family in my current world have no idea ever existed moved front and center for many years, a talented young woman that I left in the suburbs in the early '70s, eventually abandoned but never quite forgotten.

But it was probably Defender Betty, the person who came into being at Gregory Gardens, who saved the other parts of me, eventually. This is the "me" who took over our lives at that point and who, apparently, still runs the show.

I GUESS I ALWAYS envisioned that when I hit 50, I'd be an older lady and I would get out my purple shawl and collect my Social Security check. And my kids would all leave home at different times because they were spread out, they were not all bunched up age-wise. But instead, I found myself one summer living in a four-bedroom, two-bathroom house out in the suburbs with a swimming pool in the backyard, and I was all by myself.

Mel had moved out of our Walnut Creek home, eventually to live in the back office of our record store in Berkeley. Rick was living in a rented apartment in Berkeley, while 17-year-old Bob was spending the summer hitchhiking across Canada and David was doing work-study in Switzerland. He'd gone with a young friend from Berkeley High School on a student exchange program, so they were gone. Dorian was by now living at a boarding school for the mentally handicapped in Marin County.

That was the year that I was elected by the people in my congressional district to serve as a George McGovern delegate to the Democratic National Convention in Miami. So I went to Miami, leaving an empty house, and when I came back I didn't know what I was going to do. I had no models ahead of me for what life was like for older women. I was still relatively young and active, but when the kids leave home, you are supposed to be an older lady, I thought.

MEL AND I HAD separated years before, but our union refused to truly die. We'd grown apart as a couple but were both clinging to our parental roles, and trying hard to be respectful friends. I knew little of his life, or of the fact that he'd begun to lose everything of value over a period of several awful years. His desperation led him into regular weekend trips to the gambling tables in Reno and huge losses that eventually robbed him of everything he'd built over all of a lifetime.

Rick was now 21. His homosexuality was by now a huge factor and, I later learned from him, he was cutting school and spending his days wandering the streets of San Francisco in Haight-Ashbury, exploring the underside of the gay lifestyle that would later take over his life. The indignities suffered at school because of his skin color were now replaced by gay-bashing as a young adult. This was complicated by the fact that he was working for his dad at our Berkeley store on weekends and witnessing Mel's other life, a life that involved other women and the high life of being a handsome and important concert promoter and manager of the renowned

107

Edwin Hawkins Singers—the Oakland-based, nationally known gospel group—as well as a successful merchant and entrepreneur.

I remember one terrifying night when the telephone rang and it was Rick rasping out, "I'm in a phone booth across the street from the store, Mom. I'm gonna kill him!" He was talking about Mel. My son was obviously spaced out on alcohol and out of his mind with rage! I was terrified and helpless, and 15 miles away in Walnut Creek. I spent the next hour talking him down and silently, desperately praying to some unknown God.

My life separate from Mel was still relatively tolerable. I'd become a pillar of my Unitarian church, with a host of friends. I was deeply involved in the Civil Rights Movement, and was filling the empty spaces with songwriting and social action. It was easy to shut out the difficulties in my personal life in busyness, and I did. Leaving my marriage was not an option, since the indelible mandate of a Catholic ceremony had sealed my fate and my parents' dominance over that fate could not be challenged. At that time, there had not been a divorce in the family. My father was adamant. I was compliant. Foolish when I think back on it, but lives have been guided by less, I suppose. And after all, a woman's role was to tolerate a man's excesses, and by and large, Mel had been good to me and rarely abusive. This satisfied the bargain as far as my folks were concerned. My expectations were limited and he had lived up to most of them. Sound familiar?

There was a long period when I knew that I would eventually be divorced, but that period coincided with one of inertia, emotional paralysis. I was still defined by my roles of wife and mother, with the missing part being that of woman. After being married so young and then for so long, the thought of stepping off into independence was too frightening to seriously consider. So I sat and lived in the land of "What if" and "If I'd only" and postponed decisions day after disconsolate day. I convinced myself that there was only one man in my life, ever, and that I'd failed him miserably.

Taking a job seemed the only answer after years of child-rearing, and finally trying to make decisions about how to spend the rest of my life as a single adult woman.

It was around this time that I received a visit at my home from a Treasury Department agent.

"Mrs. Betty Reid?" he asked me at the door.

"Yes."

"Mrs. Melvin A. Reid?"

"Yes."

He then presented me with an official document that announced that our beautiful home of over 20 years in Walnut Creek was being seized for nonpayment of income taxes and asked me to "be off the premises" within a certain number of days, "at which time it will be placed on the market for sale."

I had continued to sign our income tax forms every year, even after Mel and I were no longer living together—I'd never had the courage not to—but I'd had no idea that those taxes had not been paid for an unknown period of years. Mel had systematically gone through every cent and every piece of property we'd owned, which at one point was a single-family home in Walnut Creek, a small duplex in Berkeley, and a newly built commercial building that housed our business in Berkeley. This had been an estate meant for our legacy, for the kids. Gone. Everything gambled away.

I'm certain that Rick had known all and held the secret since he'd worked closely with his father in the store since he was a teenager. How I wished he'd shared that burden, but how could he have? It must have been almost unbearable for him.

Mel hadn't made a mortgage payment on the record shop building for over three years. The human support system that he had had was gone. I was gone. Paul Reid, his uncle who had come into the business with Mel and built up the gospel side of it, was gone. Paul died of tuberculosis at a fairly young age, I guess he was in his early 50s. Mel couldn't pull it off. He couldn't maintain it by himself. And it failed. Everything went out from under him. And his health now failed as well. He developed diabetes, which I think was to some extent very stress related.

Fortunately, I was able to save the record store and the building that housed it, though not our beautiful house and property in Walnut Creek. By that time, though, I had met my second husband.

I WAS TAKING A midlife career-changing seminar at the Unitarian church in Walnut Creek around that time, and the leader of the seminar came to me as the course was ending to tell me that he had accepted a position as the chief administrator of a project at the University of California and wondered if I'd like to come along as part of his staff. The research project was called Project Community. It was being created to study the raging drug culture and to develop drug-prevention programs for teens. This was around 1968. The flower children had taken over the Haight-Ashbury district of San Francisco, and exploration of altered states was dominating the youth culture.

My response to his proposal was "I tell you what, I'll come to work for you for two weeks. You don't have to pay me. And if I like it, I'll stay, and if I don't like it, I won't." I mean, that's not the way you get a job, but, for reasons I'll never understand, he accepted that. It was the first day on that job that I met Bill, the man that I later married.

He was the principal investigator, and I was hired as an administrative assistant to the director of the program. William F. Soskin, Ph.D., my Bill, was an eminent psychologist, a graduate of the University of Michigan at Ann Arbor, a clinical researcher and professor of psychology at the University of Chicago, an associate professor at Harvard, and then most recently associated with the National Institute on Drug Abuse in Washington, D.C., and a member of a think tank that advised presidents John F. Kennedy and Lyndon Johnson. He was a Polish academic originally from Michigan, and though we were both born in the same part of the country,[6] we were from entirely different worlds. But within a matter of a few weeks, he and I were an item. It was quick, and it was an answer.

---

6   *EDITOR'S NOTE:* Although Betty Soskin's life is most associated with the San Francisco Bay Area and her Louisiana roots, she was actually born in Detroit, Michigan, where she spent a brief period of her early life.

I didn't ever go back home to that empty house in Walnut Creek that our family had shared through years of both pain and pleasure. I finally took up the courage to defy my Catholic family and divorced Mel. I began to stay in Berkeley, where I entered an entirely new life as a faculty spouse at the university. I didn't reconnect with the old life I had lived on the bay side of the hills, but instead entered a brand-new world. It was like Bill was the "new page" I'd turned without much thought, only reflex born of confusion.

And in time, Bill and I were married and moved in together in a lovely home atop the Berkeley hills on Grizzly Peak Boulevard, high above the university, where many of the faculty members lived, far removed from the Flatlands, the main portion of Berkeley where I had spent so much of my childhood and the first years of my first marriage. The marriage to Bill lasted 10 years and was a fascinating if unlikely period of my life that in these final years of mine now seems almost a fantasy.

I loved Bill, just as I had loved my first husband, Mel. And just like with Mel, there were sacrifices that came with that love. For one thing, I stopped writing music after I married Bill.

I had begun to compose music during the troubled years of my marriage to Mel and the various difficulties surrounding the raising of my four children. Though untrained, I was writing songs in my head. I taught myself to play guitar by ear so that I could reproduce the chords that appeared in my mind without hesitation or design. The instrument was so responsive to even my unschooled demands. I never went back and tried to change these compositions or polish them up. I continued to write music that way, unpretentiously and as naturally as if trained.

One must remember, though, that it was in those years at the end of the 1960s that so many of the poets, singers, performers of every kind were daring to speak their truths through music. In such venues as coffeehouses and performing cafés, street musicians were popping up everywhere and bringing their art to a world in chaos. Nothing about my creating or performing was unusual, so I simply thought of myself as "making up songs." The word *composing* was beyond, way beyond, my imagination.

But during my second marriage, it was only to be for a brief time.

I remember one night when I was so excited about a piece I had just made up. I ran downstairs with my guitar in hand, into the library where Bill was working on a grant proposal. I burst into the room with the words "You've got to listen to this!" I sat down with my bare feet tucked in between the sofa cushions and started to sing my just-born latest, most beautiful song, and he listened. He really did listen. As I sang the last note he said, "You know, you are *so good*, Betty. I think I can get you into the Music Department as a special student at the university, and you can learn how the *real* composers do it. The *joy* you're going to have when you get this really polished up." Feeling disappointed and slightly hurt, I said, "No! It's complete. If I try to do that, it's going to turn into something else, because 20 minutes from now I'm going to feel differently. *This* is what I felt five minutes ago upstairs. It *can't* be changed."

But he had completely blown my confidence. I went back upstairs and for the first time I said to myself, "I'm not composing. This is not how real composers do it." It felt as though what I was doing amounted to little more than child's play. It was of little importance to anyone but me. And I stopped composing music, and never wrote another song.

I think the importance in that is that this isn't just how we turn off children and their joy in the learning and creative processes, this is how we turn off adults as well. I feel teary even thinking about it now, because it shut down the poet in me. It squeezed out in other ways, in my writing, for example. Whatever it was that had enabled those talents had to find someplace to go, and so it found its way into my computer, into my blog, into the Internet, into the homes of strangers across the world. It found a way to bleed into life the hidden parts of myself.

I RECEIVED AN ALARMING phone call from Rick, pleading for help. He'd arrived at work at the record store in Berkeley that morning to find his dad lying on the floor in a coma in the back office, where he had been living for months. Rick was terrified! No one knew that Mel had been diagnosed as diabetic. He was a former athlete who'd taken particularly good care of his health for all the years that I'd known him. I hardly recognized this helpless, disheveled bearded man who lay so still and helpless, his body so awkwardly twisted, that morning. None of us knew how long he'd been in that state.

It was then that I first learned just how much Mel's life had deteriorated, how awful was the state of the business, and just how totally the store had descended to street level.

Sacramento Street had become ground zero for the sale of illegal drugs, and our little store was right in the middle of that drug trade that stretched from Richmond to the north through Oakland to the south. The street corners were peopled by young dealers plying their trade night and day. Occasional shootouts had become a part of the new normal. Police actions were constant.

In the early days of that transition from a low-income black community to a crime capital, Mel went to the police station to try to get help. He was told by the desk assigned to community affairs that "we like to have districts like yours. When something happens in other parts of Berkeley we usually know where we can pick up the culprits!"

Eventually, Mel gave up and, to some extent, the record shop had morphed into this new reality. There were water pipes for pot smoking in the display cases that had once sported only the latest in black music, and velvet-embossed posters suitable for being shown under black light—symbolic of the drug culture of the day—hung on the walls for sale.

Mel was helpless against this new reality, and became its saddest casualty in a phenomenon that was showing up in the inner cities throughout the nation.

But all of that was diffused by the awfulness of the situation with Mel's health that was at hand. The fears were swept away in those moments as I rushed past our terrified son to try to revive Mel and then to call an ambulance that would carry him off to the nearest emergency room. Within hours, Mel's right leg would be amputated at the knee and Bill and I would be standing over his bed in the ICU, waiting for him to awaken from the anesthesia to discover this tragic truth. This was the first time my two husbands met.

Fortunately for us, the *psychologist* Bill was standing beside me in all of his professionalism, and was able to deftly guide the three of us through those critical first hours of this family tragedy. Dr. William F. Soskin could not have been more loving or helpful. His generosity with his expertise, his compassion, and his ability and willingness to support us in all ways was beyond expectations. I could not have felt more deeply loved, or less ready to incorporate the demands of the caretaking of a former husband into my new life with Bill. But fortunately, the old friendship Mel and I had shared as youngsters returned to see us through, and a new relationship formed in place of the old failed marriage.

In the days immediately following the crisis of Mel's tragic life, I found myself driving to South Berkeley and into what was now a crime-ridden and poverty-stricken community. It was time to try to assess next moves.

It was clear that there was little carryover from those early days when I'd been the principal player, with Rick in his playpen and those orange crates we'd started with, while Mel worked elsewhere. That was gone. The experience was now buried beneath years of child-rearing and suburban living, political activities and the beginnings of university life.

Besides all that, I was terrified of the environment in which I now found myself. African American life at this level was as alien to me as suburban life had been some years before. The stories learned from Rick rocked my entire being. What had become normal in the life of the store was beyond my wildest and most fearsome dreams. The billboards along the street almost universally featured liquor ads. There were 12 places where one could purchase alcohol within a six-block stretch. There were street corner "offices" manned by young black males who guarded them fiercely. Across the street from our business stood an old house that was obviously being used for prostitution, and our windows looked out on those activities constantly. There was a camper that parked across the street and served as a floating gambling operation.

Reid's Records had as many lives as I did, in a lot of ways. It started off as a little R&B and jazz kind of spot that grew way past its potential and did very well. Then it went through a period of becoming a growing gospel shop. Then it found its level with the street. All that time, the street was going down. Sacramento Street eventually became sort of the sin capital of the city of Berkeley.

The year that I came back after Mel's health failed, when I went in to close the store down, what had started out as a successful record store had become a head shop. It had become what the street was. I didn't know what to do with it when I first came back. There were mainstream record stores opening up around the UC Berkeley campus—within short driving distance from our shop—that were selling black-oriented music at a discount that our record store had once had the exclusive market for. There was no way I could compete with them. But the shop still had a clientele of church people whom no one else was serving. So I cut out everything but gospel, because the mainstream white market hadn't discovered it yet.

Now the store was mine, but I knew that there was no way to make a financial success of it anymore. If you were going to make it into the Fortune 500, it was highly unlikely that you'd do it through a small black-music store on Sacramento Street in Berkeley, California, in the 1970s. It was necessary to establish new goals if even mere survival in this particular marketplace was going to be possible.

I was a different person than I'd been when I worked behind the counter at the record shop in the first years of my marriage to Mel. I'd found a role in the Black Revolution in the 1960s. I was married to a white university professor now, and working at the university myself. I considered myself a social activist and had become very political. I decided to keep the record shop and use it toward achieving social change. If it paid its own expenses as well as a couple of salaries for someone to work for me, that would be all right with me. So the shop gave rise to another life that was almost not related to its first life.

There was a foreclosure notice posted on the front door when I arrived at the shop that first day. I called the mortgage company and asked them for an extension, then called the record distributors and told them that it looked like there might still be a life there, and that if they gave me about six months, maybe I could pull it off. There was cooperation from everybody. With their help, I was able to bring the old record shop back to life, and revive old relationships toward a new beginning.

But the place was redlined.[7] I couldn't get any insurance on the building. There were things that seemed impossible to deal with, but I learned how to deal with them. I learned how to cope. I was told that there was no way that the banks or finance companies could do anything for me—no second mortgages, no loans, no nothing. But if I could pick up the building and move it six blocks in either direction, they might be able to help me. Because of where it was sitting, there was nobody who would write an insurance policy for me or grant a loan.

So I changed the community that the shop building was sitting in.

I'd been political pretty much without intending to be political. I'm convinced that politics is just a part of life and for me it's really integrated. When I was much younger I had visions of changing the world, but I finally got so that I broke it down to

---

7   *EDITOR'S NOTE:* In places and times where outright segregation of the races was illegal, redlining was the process used by banks and mortgage and real estate companies through the early 1970s or so to unofficially divide communities between white and black. The term almost certainly comes from the practice of drawing, on backroom city maps, red lines around areas in which black residents and businesses were to be confined. Outside the redline boundaries, blacks found it difficult or impossible to purchase property or open businesses. Inside the redline boundaries, where most blacks were confined, banks and mortgage companies deemed it too "risky" to put in too much money for loans to purchase or upgrade businesses or home properties, and insurance companies often refused to issue policies or priced them unreasonably high.

500 feet, and everything within that 500 feet was going to have to shape up. So I would have a problem, and I would simply try to figure out how that particular problem gets solved, not necessarily how it fit into a greater whole. I would go to Berkeley City Hall and see whomever I had to see to get something changed. So my work politically was very much integrated with my work on the needs of the record shop.

Shortly after I took over the building, either the city or the local bus company, AC Transit, installed a bus bench directly in the front of the store, only a few inches away from the store's eight-foot-tall plate glass windows. The young drug dealers used that bench, and all of the other benches up and down Sacramento Street, as their offices. Here's where the deals were made and duels were fought.

I kept sending letters to the City Council and the Planning Commission telling them about the problem and asking that the bench in front of my shop be removed. Every time I did that, the answer I got back was "These benches were put in at the will of the community. And the only way they can come out—because they are part of the city-approved beautification project—is if the community comes together and says, 'Take them out.' Otherwise, under no circumstances can we do so."

One day, I came to work and somebody had skipped the curve in the street and hit this bench with their car, and the bench was hopelessly smashed. I picked up the phone, called the public services department and told them about the bench and said, "You know, I don't want it fixed, just take it away. I do *not* want it repaired."

Within the next three days, every bench along Sacramento Street in an eight-block stretch surrounding the shop was gone. Apparently the city's public services department had heard what I was saying all the time, but because of the way I was demanding that they change, I had been publicly putting the City in the position of having to tell me no. And that's when I began to learn how things really happen politically and how one has to be strategic.

Bɪʟʟ Soꜱᴋɪɴ ʜᴀᴅ ᴅᴇᴠᴇʟᴏᴘᴇᴅ a drug-prevention program called Project Community at UC Berkeley. It employed us both, and we were working on five high school sites. Besides myself, the staff was made up of a group of doctoral candidates from the UC Psychology Department. Bill combined them with a group of artists to work with high school students in these special programs on each of these campuses. I started out in the administration and ended up, before it was over, co-leading groups in the schools with those studying psychology at the university. It was a real learning experience for me.

That experience with Project Community was completely different from anything I'd ever lived through in my entire life, because Bill's world was a very different one. It was different, but in many ways, it was the same.

One thing that was the same was the prescribed roles of wives. I remember one dinner party in academia where it all came together for me. Bill was a brilliant man, and he had brilliant theories. And in order for him to be able to make certain points about those theories, he would toss me lines that I was supposed to reply to in a certain way in order to move the discussion around to where he wanted it to go. It was scripted.

I remember we were at a party in Orinda that was being held for a very well-known visiting psychologist who had a beautiful wife, whose role it was to maneuver the conversation around to her husband's latest theory. I sat fascinated while listening to "the game," so when Bill tried the same thing, I remember stubbornly not participating and Bill becoming more and more irritated because I wouldn't move the conversation the way he wanted it to go.

On the way home, I told him I would never attend another one of those parties. That was the first time I began to see a whole level of interplay between the sexes in the academic world that I had had no way to even be aware of before I became an academic wife.

I also saw a lot of hypocrisy in academia that was not unlike what I had known in other contexts. I think I had rather naïvely believed that the greater the intelligence, the greater the ethical sense, and that turned out not to bear up under the close scrutiny of a marriage.

Coupled with being on the campus as a part of academic life, the opportunity to go back into the ghetto, to go back to South Berkeley, was thrust upon me. I was living a fascinating life as a faculty wife, while also driving down from the hills each day to be a businesswoman in the black community. And that eventually became impossible to reconcile. I had lived most of my life on a bridge interpreting one side for the other. The whole time I was in Walnut Creek, I was telling white folks what the black folks meant, and black folks what the white folks meant. I was doing this bridge thing. That's the way I sensed my life's role in those transformative years. I'd accepted that, and it had worked for me for a while.

When I came back to run the record shop on my own, I found myself more and more using what I found in the white community to make things work in the black community. Eventually I couldn't do both. I had to make a choice. I had to decide which side of that line I was going to be on. That's when I really became black. The work to be done in the black community had to be facilitated by my other life in the white community and academia, but I couldn't stay up there on the hill and do the work down on Sacramento Street. I had to be both in and of the black community.

WE WERE RENTING TO tenants on the second floor above the record shop, and there was one man up there especially who was giving me a great deal of trouble, and who I believed might be contributing to the drug problem going on out along Sacramento Street. He was politically involved in the community and was well known at City Hall as an important black leader in South Berkeley.

It was approaching election time in Berkeley. I met with Shirley Dean, a white Berkeley city council member who was running for mayor, and asked for her help in dealing with the drug problem on the street around the shop and with this problem tenant in particular. Ms. Dean told me she was sorry, but the tenant I was speaking of was someone who could deliver votes in South Berkeley's black community, and she couldn't afford to work against him with the election coming up. She refused to help me.

Shirley Dean was in a race against a black man, Gus Newport. Though I'd not met Newport at the time, I went back to my community, which was Dean's political territory, and plastered my building with Gus Newport signs. Then I went up and down the street to all the other merchants and delivered my candidate's signs. I figured that I had sorely needed her help, and she hadn't offered any. That left me nothing to do but work against her in the election. It was just that simple. Gus Newport won that election, and I eventually evicted the problem tenant from the building.

And that's the first time I flexed my political muscles and something happened, and I began to see how I could move things politically, if I did so strategically.

I got myself hired as aide to one of the Berkeley city councilmen, Don Jelinek. And though I continued to operate the store in South Berkeley, I worked as Don's aide through several years and two terms of office, putting me on the fifth floor of Berkeley City Hall right in the center of where things get down and power is generated.

Every day I would go to City Hall to put in my time in Don's office. I would sit in staff meetings, planning for the city council meetings and the agendas, and learn all about that process. I also could sit in on any other kind of meetings I wanted to. I regularly attended city council meetings and really began to learn how city government works. It provided a priceless education for a would-be community organizer, though I didn't know what that term meant at the time.

Mayor Gus Newport appointed me to a task force that was assigned to find scattered site housing throughout the city to build 50 low-income homes. I tried to get the city to take over the run-down crack house–and–squatter properties across Sacramento Street from our store as one of the sites. I was able to convince them that it was cancerous to the rest of the city. If we would change that, I said, all the property in the area would become more valuable. The city didn't make it a part of the original project, but they did eventually take over those rundown Sacramento Street properties as a separate project. They invested $8.5 million in it, bought up the properties, and tore down the old houses. They ended up building 49 units of new housing. It's called the

Byron Rumford Plaza after the black California assemblyman from Berkeley who authored the state's first and most important fair-housing law. But the Rumford Plaza will always be known as Betty's houses to my kids.

The face of the community was forever changed. That area of Sacramento Street in Berkeley became a whole different place. And that was the beginning of my political/social activity in Berkeley.

When new political opportunities came up, I took advantage of them. When one of my friends, Dion Aroner, held the office of assemblywoman for the 14th Assembly District, I filled in for a young African American man she'd hired as her field representative but had to let go. I staffed one of the satellite offices in the Richmond area, and found myself back in the saddle. I really thought that I was only coming in as a temporary placeholder until a permanent replacement could be hired, because I saw myself as being in my retirement years. But instead, I got fired up again and off I went. I ended up working that position with Dion as well as with her successor, Loni Hancock.

That work allowed me to build support for a number of widely varied interests while representing the Assembly member elected from Berkeley, Richmond to the north, and several smaller communities in between. One of these projects was completely unexpected—working as a consultant in the early stages of what later became the Rosie the Riveter/WWII Home Front National Historical Park in Richmond.

ALTHOUGH I HAD STOPPED composing my own music by that point, my interest in music had by no means disappeared. And so, during the '90s I came to serve as a self-appointed interim co-director of the Nu Upper Room, an important, innovative performing arts venue in the Fruitvale district of East Oakland.

It happened by sheer accident.

One of my music store customers was a fascinating young-ish, dreadlocked, green-eyed, light-skinned, handsome, and proud African American man from San Francisco. He called himself Rafiq Bilal, and appeared to be a gentle revolutionary. He stopped in the shop one day, wanting to sell a two-volume videotaped set of *The Story of Africa*. At that time I maintained the only location in the Bay Area that specialized in the rental of African American videos. It was a fateful meeting. I instantly and intuitively recognized him as someone I would love to know, and indeed I did in a friendship that grew and flourished over the next several years.

The Nu Upper Room at that time was an interesting gathering place in the South of Market area of San Francisco. It had evolved out of a drug-treatment program that Rafiq had directed at Reverend Cecil Williams's Glide Memorial Church in the Tenderloin. It served as an evening meeting place for members of the recovery community, where there would be fewer temptations to relapse back into the underworld of abuse. Rafiq created a place where poets, writers, playwrights, rappers, singers, and dancers came together in an informal collective where they could share their work in an atmosphere free of drugs and alcohol, and be safe.

Over time, young people from around the Bay Area stumbled upon the place and slowly took it over and began to form a loosely connected artists' showcase where visiting musicians and artists joined with young people, mentorships started to form, and the arts flourished. The young had also yearned for a safe place for themselves in a world increasingly enveloped in the darkness of addictions of one kind or another, and they soon outnumbered those first participants and it became their "in" place.

As it is with places where young people of color begin to collect in significant numbers, the San Francisco police eventually grew suspicious and their harassment forced this incubator for exciting new arts to relocate outside of the city, across the bay, in an old, crumbling Masonic temple in the Fruitvale district in Oakland. It was here that I first visited this remarkable collection of young people in full bloom.

With no more than colorfully designed flyers scattered in high school campus parking lots and tacked on telephone poles and slipped behind windshield wipers around the Bay Area, literally hundreds of young people would come together in that leaky old building—with code violations galore and few fire exits—for concerts and hip-hop poetry jams. Young graffiti artists using large brushes painted from buckets onto four-by-eight-foot panels of Sheetrock to the sounds of live experimental jazz as young dancers improvised to the music. It was a period of the most exciting arts movement one could ever witness or dare to be a part of.

Not too long after I was first introduced to this magical place, Rafiq Bilal suffered a massive stroke and was hospitalized in the local county hospital. The Nu Upper Room family was demoralized for weeks before Jennifer Ross, Sister Shakiri of Zaccho Dance Theatre, and I began to alternate as a group of "den mothers"—kind of emergency interim artistic directors—as a way to keep the place open and operating long enough to find answers to where it might be moved and nurtured into the full-blown movement we each recognized it to be. We knew intuitively that here was something precious and important, if only we could protect it long enough for others to know.

I often sat in that darkened hall to listen to Amiri Baraka read from his latest works, Steve Coleman lead jam sessions that grew from informal jazz workshops, young rappers express the new cadence and body movements, competing in the telling of the stories of their lives and peoples, dancers and choreographers testing new materials, then-obscure but now–internationally known visual artist and photographer Keba Konte, older blues singers and monologists working together with upcoming young performers. We saw a reunion of the Last Poets of the '60s and the early days of the great jazz group Mingus Amungus. Gradually, the age groups shifted to be more inclusive and Robert Henry Johnson—at one time one of the Alvin Ailey dancers—and his mother—a former San Francisco nightclub singer—appeared together one evening before an audience of hundreds. Shakiri, a playwright of note, presented new works, and Will Power, one of the young guiding lights of the Nu Upper Room, six foot three inches of lanky, richly talented San Francisco performance artist, would present solo pieces that were astounding in their perception and sheer brilliance. If there had been a board overseeing the Nu Upper Room, Will would have surely been considered its chairman, and Rafiq's protégé.

I sat one night and watched a young man from India in what looked like Punjabi dress playing a piano, and he was playing Thelonious Monk's "'Round Midnight" on the battered piano. Rafiq's young son, Mohammed Bilal, was doing rapping, I think, and there were three amazing young women of unidentifiable racial background dancing to the music. And I'm sitting in this huge space and looking around it, and realizing that there was no effort involved in creating racial equality. That group in that room worked together around art. They were not together around race or trying to rise out of race or to compensate in some way for their differences. That same night, a young Native American rapped the story of his people. The things that I saw in that building—my age didn't matter. I was certainly not trying to be young. I've never tried to be young as such, or found aging a limiting factor. But age wasn't even a problem. There were people there, certainly not as old as I, but in their 40s and 50s, who were there as artists. I saw young rap artists who were simply phenomenal, but they weren't there at the Upper Room because they were black or white, they were there because they were artists. Trying to put that together, these kids, they'd accomplished something that the people across town were still working hard to achieve, without realizing *it had already happened.*

But even so, the other thing that was fascinating about the Upper Room was that here was a place that was built on black culture. Everyone who was involved did not have to be black, that wasn't the point. But black culture was the basis of *everything* that was going on there. The gurus were largely black. The people who came there, the white people who came there, the Indian people who came there, the Native Americans, the Latinos, the Filipino people who came there, came there to participate in black culture. It was simply amazing, because it was so clearly identified.

The local Oakland police, fully aware of our activities that ran late into the night on many occasions, were totally supportive of our presence despite those clear code violations and the significant weekend noise. They often stopped by in plain clothes during their off-duty hours to participate in these underground activities.

Unlike San Francisco, the Oakland officers were wonderful about looking the other way in order to protect our late-night partying. Those same police in a different time but in the same place were in a constant struggle to quell the automobile sideshows conducted out on Oakland's streets that were seen by an unknowing community as a scourge upon the city. Little do they realize what was lost or how different it all might have been had they known and nurtured the Nu Upper Room and its collective of creative artists.

In time, the blossoming of something I saw as just as significant as the flower-child period of the Haight was forced to disband. This alcohol-and-drug-free oasis of an environment that was producing such exciting art must soon be abandoned due to the impending redevelopment of the Fruitvale district and our inability to meet the really tiny amount of money needed to continue occupying the disintegrating 100-year-old building.

After its closure, that talented collection of extraordinary young artists was scattered to the winds. I tried vainly to find a building to drop over them, but failed miserably. Despite years of building goodwill with the Berkeley city government, I could get no one to listen. Gradually those young people of the Nu Upper Room began to disappear to Southern California. The most dedicated moved on to New York, where they continued to mature into their arts as performers of note.

Imagine my amazement when, years later, while watching Charlie Rose interviewing leading intellectuals and theologians Bill and Judith Moyers on the eve of the airing of the first segment of their new 10-week PBS series Bill Moyers on Faith and Reason, suddenly onscreen was none other than handsome, brilliant "35-year-old Will Power," as described by Judith Moyers. He had emerged into a full-fledged New York playwright with an off-Broadway show based on the Oedipus myth, but done in hip hop. A snippet from his upcoming segment had him seated across from Moyers in a one-on-one, being interviewed and treated with the same riveted attention as that bestowed upon the late Joseph Campbell or Salman Rushdie. I was stunned! And oh, how affirmed I felt! The world was now ready to see what I'd seen those years ago, but for so many it was too late.

WHEN WE FIRST BEGAN dating, Bill had told me, "You know that I'm studying Buddhism. I don't know at what point it will be, but when the time comes I will be required to enter the monastery and be in total isolation for three years. That has been my ambition for many years. I must complete my studies. You must understand that."

And then when things got serious between us, he deposited $5,000 in the local bank and handed me the bankbook with my name at the top. Enclosed was a note. "These funds will always be here. It is your security, to be used if and when appropriate. You can feel free to move on at any time. You'll know now whether you're here because you want to be. Meanwhile, will you marry me?"

We agreed then that at such time that he felt the need to enter the part of his training that required the period of isolation, we would divorce. Since neither of us could be sure just who would return from such an experience—and since neither of us felt that I should be confined to living in my own version of isolation because of the demands of his religious practice—we would come together at that point and renegotiate our relationship. And we would do all of that legally, so that he could feel free to move on, deeper into his religious experience, if that's where life led, and so that I could continue my own life without him, or with someone else. We would spend the year before his departure working out the legal plans and consulting with a good therapist.

We did all of that. When it came Bill's time to enter the Buddhist monastery, we divorced. Four years later, he passed away at the age of 72.

AFTER A TUMULTUOUS AND painful adolescence, at 21 Rick had moved to Berkeley from Walnut Creek, into his first apartment. He was on his own. The call came, the one I'd expected all our lives. "Mom, can you come to dinner next Wednesday? Dress your prettiest. It's something special." When I arrived that evening, he announced that he had something terribly important to tell me. It was at that moment that he told me about Ron, a handsome (white) man in his early 30s and owner of a kind of Sharper Image–type store in San Francisco.

"He wants me to move in with him as his roommate, Mom."

"And will you?" asked I.

"But you don't understand, Mom."

"Yes, I do," says I.

"You've always known, haven't you?" says Rick.

"Yes."

We left to join Ron at a fine restaurant, where he announced that he and Rick were planning a trip to Amsterdam soon, and that he'd not wanted to take off without our family knowing about their relationship. I felt relieved and grateful that we'd together crossed some threshold that freed us all. We'd all come out, that evening.

But all that's left of that relationship are a few shares of Ford Motor Company stock given to Rick as a Christmas present years ago. The documents have been in my safe deposit box for all these years—a box I thought I'd closed out long ago when I moved. Rick had a key and placed them there in a sober moment, I guess. I knew nothing of them until recently, when they appeared in my name in an announcement from the State of California of unclaimed property, the last vestige of a lost life.

It had been a day of changes. I'd decided to sell the home in El Cerrito. I'd bought it 10 years before in order to accommodate my mother's last days. Dad had died at 92 in 1986. Mother survived him by nine years, to the age of 101. Eventually, she'd passed on and the cost of maintaining "a house that could accommodate the Christmas tree" could no longer be justified.

I'd located a one-bedroom condo in Richmond's Hilltop Village and was in the process of crating up all the "stuff" that would go into storage when the call came. It was Rick's landlord. "Mrs. Soskin, we haven't seen your son for three weeks, and there is growing concern among his neighbors that . . ." My heart stopped for a fraction of a second, and I could hardly catch my breath.

I sent David to Rick's apartment, knowing that I couldn't drive across town to learn the truth. I sat and waited with a growing feeling of numbness, my body magically preparing to protect itself against what was sure to come. The phone pierced the silence with a shrill ring and the landlord's voice on the line with "I'm so sorry, Mrs. Soskin." I screamed! David hadn't reached me yet. He'd opted to drive to tell me in person rather than to speak those fateful words by phone, knowing that I was alone. David's words are now engraved on my brain: "It's over, Mom. It's over." How difficult, even now, to admit that embedded in the horror and pain of grief lurked the feeling of relief. He was right. It was over.

This wasn't new. There was a familiarity about this strange mixture of feelings. It was a reminder that in 1987 and within three short months, the key men in my life had all passed away. My father first of all, then Mel, then Bill. In those terrible three months, I was at first devastated with grief. I'd been at the foot of my father's bed at the hospital when I heard his last breath being expelled. Bill lay in a coma for months before the end came. Mel died after years of living as an amputee, a living death for a former athlete.

Imagine my surprise to find that, only a few months after the deaths of those three men, right behind the grief lay the exultation of emancipation. As it is with many women in my age group, I'd been consistently defined by the men I'd loved for an entire lifetime, and without question. I'd had no sense of my individuality, my womanness, before their deaths. I would never have wished their deaths. I would never have purchased my freedom with their deaths. But following their deaths, the grief mixed with a strange sense of relief, and the two feelings rolled over me in successive waves, one preceding the other, over and over. How many months I lived in that space of silent joyful/sadness I'm not sure.

In the last two decades of his life, Rick had partnered with his soulmate, Gordon Higgins, with whom he would share his life in a monogamous "marriage" for 19 uninterrupted years of torment and pain. They were codependent alcoholics. They died about a year apart. I wonder—had they survived—if today's judgment by the California courts making same-sex marriages legal might have saved them? Being same-sex, of different races, and members of a despised minority on both scores, would it have been different now?

I remember the day that Gordon died while Rick was at work. Gordon had been suffering from lung cancer. Rick had called me earlier that morning to ask if I'd look in on Gordon, if I had the time, since ". . . he didn't look terribly well." Rick later came to my office, two blocks from their apartment, after calling to break the news that Gordon had died, and we went to their place together and arrived just as the coroner was picking up Gordon's body. We then entered a nightmare when Rick called Maine to let Gordon's family know of the death. They slammed the phone down in his face! They refused to accept responsibility for the disposal of the body, even though we were not asking this, but also refused to release the remains to us for burial. It was dreadful.

It would be 30 days before the coroner's office would release the body to us. Rick knew for all that time that Gordon was lying on a cold marble slab in the coroner's office in Martinez, the Contra Costa County seat. Rick had no legal status through which to claim the body before that time, the law requiring that period before Gordon's remains could be declared abandoned. Then and only then could we have Gordon cremated and his ashes scattered as he had wished.

And now my beloved Rick had died. And those feelings of intense grief mixed with quiet relief had returned.

Rick had been dead on his bathroom floor for three weeks when his body was found. He'd died of cirrhosis from years of alcoholism. He'd died alone. His death followed Gordon's by no more than a year. He had never really recovered from the pain of the experience of Gordon's death. He had no wish to live. Rick's death had been one of the longest acts of thinly veiled suicide imaginable, a slow, inescapable descent into the hell of self-destruction. David described it right. Rick's life had never really started. A bright potential had been snuffed out years before for a variety of reasons, some beyond my understanding, some not. I'll never know how much I contributed to that despite all the love invested. None of us can ever know that, and it's probably just as well.

Fortunately, both Bob and David had a sense of having reached Rick a few months before his death, at a time when he was hospitalized in crisis. His blood pressure had risen to dangerous levels and though close to death, he'd survived for the moment. Both younger brothers had spent time visiting with him in the hospital. Though we hadn't given it words, I suspect that we each knew that he'd not live much longer.

Knowing doesn't soften the shock or finality of death at all. Nor do the lost lives of those who went before. Each loss is all-consuming. Experience does little to prepare one for losing a loved one, though as we age there is some movement toward the acceptance of one's own ending. A child cannot imagine nonexistence. I can. Maturity may be measured by just when we accept the fact that we must die as all beings do, and the emphasis begins to center on just how well we are using and have used the privilege of life. A friend said to me on the occasion of my mother's death, "Remember, Betty, no life is complete without a death." He'll never know how important those words would become in my own struggle with the acceptance of my own mortality. Being all used up before the end has become a driving force—an obsession. The growing sense of urgency has added spice to my days and lightness to my step in this most recent decade, when life has become more precious than ever before.

I think of the plight of all those hopeful gays and lesbians on the day they camped out at San Francisco's City Hall in the hope of getting married, in those times before gay marriage was legalized in San Francisco, and then, finally, in many cities and states throughout the country. But this was long before that dam was breached. Thought of them on the day of the San Francisco City Hall gay-marriage demonstration as the heavy rains pelted down during the night. Thought of Rick, and wept in the night.

8

RICHMOND AND ROSIE AND BETTY THE RANGER

IT FEELS IRONIC TO think that my first experience with the National Park Service and the Rosie the Riveter Visitor Education Center—which later on played such a major role in my life—was at a presentation given at the local library in Richmond early in the process of establishing the park. There was a slideshow presentation with a discussion afterward intended to involve the community in the process. I was there on a work assignment as a field representative for Assembly member Dion Aroner. I felt keenly uncomfortable all through the presentation without much sense of just why that was. I had only recently moved to Richmond from Berkeley, and I didn't yet feel like a Richmond resident. In addition, I had pretty much dismissed all of my own World War II experience. I had no idea where the union hall where I had worked—a temporary building long ago torn down by that time—had been located, and the overview of the old shipyards displayed during the slideshow was new material for me. I'd not been within sight of the shipyards at any point during the war and therefore never saw a ship under construction during that time, nor even witnessed a ship launching.

When the formal presentation ended and the punch-and-cookie period had not quite started, I remember saying out loud to no one in particular, "I have such a love-hate relationship with Rosie!" Judy Hart, the newly appointed superintendent of the new park project, looked a little taken aback, but bravely asked what I meant. I then told the group about my role in the war and about how far from all of that I really felt—that I could hardly recall the war. I'd obviously forgotten it all as soon as possible, and now it was coming back, bringing all of the affect with it.

I had the distinct feeling that this new Rosie the Riveter/World War II Home Front National Historical Park was going to dredge up some troubling feelings, and that there needed to be some strategy for sorting some of that out, especially for the nonwhite people who had lived through the period.

I'd spent some of those war years as a clerk in the office of Boilermakers A-36 on Barrett Avenue, a few miles from the Kaiser Richmond Shipyards. The *A* in A-36 stood for *Auxiliary*, meaning that the unions were not yet racially integrated, and that this was a separate all-black union. It also meant that those cards that I spent those years filing in long trays held the information for all African American shipyard workers, and that I knew that "trainee" and "helper" were written after the name of every black worker. This was by agreement between the shipyards and the regular union so that at war's end, no black worker who had held an auxiliary trainee union card would be in competition with white union workers for a job when peace came.

One thing I remembered was that the population of the city of Richmond had grown by 110,000. Virtually overnight, black and white workers were brought from the Southern states to build the nation's ships to help win the nation's war. They came from the tenant farms, out of a land of Jim Crow segregation. They'd not yet shared drinking fountains, voting rights, or public accommodations, and wouldn't for another 20 years. And some of them brought the Ku Klux Klan with them as well.

I wasn't sure that the National Park Service appreciated the full impact of the fact that, in the postwar period, there had been a resurgence of the KKK in Richmond, and that cross burnings had occurred a number of times before being brought under control. There is an historic photograph of the Klan marching in full regalia down Macdonald Avenue, the main street of Richmond, in 1927. And I didn't know how, or if, this part of the city's history during and after the war years could be presented in the context of a national park honoring the home front workers.

I also wondered how a park could be created without federal lands specifically set aside for exclusive park use. How could a national park work when so many of the structures from a bygone era it was designed to commemorate either existed no more or had had their façades radically changed and their purposes altered?

While some of the war housing facilities meant for the white workers remained, all housing where nonwhites lived during the war had been torn down by the government—again by prior agreement—within weeks of the war's end. The Jim Crow union hall where I worked was on Barrett Avenue, and it met the same fate as the war housing for black folk. If the home front story was to be told through still-standing structures, I thought, one would never know that we were ever here or that we participated in that unprecedented effort that turned out a Victory ship every five days.

And then there was the tragedy of the lives of the black shipyard workers who were left to manage in a strange place with little or no government assistance once their shipyard days were over. Their shipbuilding experience was not transferrable by design, so when the war was over, it was back to those "jobs nobody else wanted." Returning to the South was not an option. When the temporary war housing was torn down, they dragged scrap wood, piping, nails, and screws from the deconstruction sites into the unincorporated area just north of the Richmond city limits and began to build lean-tos in order to go on with their lives in place. Much of the area was marshland and given to flooding. Much of the land was agricultural property previously owned by the interned Japanese and subject to being taken away at some point in the future. There was little work to be had, but they survived, and remained, and one cannot imagine a Richmond now without their presence and the presence of their offspring and descendants. That story has never been told. Would "Rosie" tell it, and how?

THE PERIOD OF World War II has always been difficult for me to call up. Never had the sense of patriotism that I saw evidenced in others. It was a time of confusion for me. I was barely 20 when the war was declared, and newly married. In the way that our minds tend to protect us, mine pretty much blotted out the pain of that time, and I only remembered it in fragments.

In the summer of 2004 I received an invitation to visit the White House and, along with others, be honored as "Rosies," women who had worked in the home front war effort. I declined the invitation. I have always hung back from these celebrations and had such painfully mixed feelings about being considered such, but other than honestly expressing my reluctance openly, I continued to smile about it and to bury the anguish. Another African American worker was chosen.

I'd spent the war filing discriminatory cards for black workers who could not rise above trainee status. And I'd done it in a Jim Crow union hall, at that. Rosies were always identified as the women who had actually worked in places like the Kaiser shipyards, actually building the ships that carried American servicemen into battle. To have myself embraced as a "Rosie" at this stage in life felt strangely inappropriate.

There seemed to be a step missing in the process. I was not even sure what that step was at the time, just that it was missing. *Maybe it was like reparations*, I thought. I needed someone to apologize, maybe, or to at least recognize that a wrong had been done to young people, like I was then. I was just as bright and capable then as now, sans some life experience that has deepened what was naturally inherent in that pretty young Betty.

I was far too "civilized" and reasonable to deal with those feelings openly in the summer of 2004. Nothing to do but try to squish them down from whence they'd come and continue to "do the work." I've spent a lifetime doing just that. I recognized it as a part of the concept of "white privilege" that is so poorly understood by most who enjoy it. It's so hard to defend against, since to attack that kind of tainted innocence seems beneath the intelligence of those of us who suffer from its effects. It's all so complicated, and so terribly old and tired.

In a way, I was finding that the creation of this national park might present the opportunity for the recollections of a war through the eyes of women—being told through their feminine stories and artifacts—that would differ significantly from the memories of men who tell their stories through body counts and the machines of wars.

I was beginning to see this work as a way to contribute to something historic. Giving up the rage might help in that process.

But I wondered if this was making any sense to anyone but me.

THROUGHOUT ALL ITS PARKS before the creation of the Rosie the Riveter park, the National Park Service told the American story through carefully selected, still-standing "structures." There is the restoration of the New England textile mills that produced the fabrics that clothed us until recent times, for example, or the restoration of the encampments where Japanese Americans were interned in that shameful period during World War II, or San Francisco's Presidio army base, where buildings that were constructed before the Civil War are still standing.

Some of those types of structures were still in place in Richmond when we began the master planning for the Rosie the Riveter/WWII Home Front National Historical Park to commemorate the lives and work of the Americans who supported that overseas war back here in the United States. There was Kaiser's Richmond Shipyard Number Three, where that horde of migrant workers was brought together to build the ships, two giant Whirley Cranes that lifted the prefabricated steel parts onto the hulls of the ships being built, the original Kaiser field hospital that was the genesis of the national HMO movement and preventive health care, the

Maritime Child Development Centers with 24-hour-a-day child care that served as the progenitor of the Head Start Program, the Kaiser shipyard cafeteria that later became the site of a community college. All of these structures would "tell the story" of the home front activity during the war years in Richmond. In addition, park organizers were planning to dedicate to the women who served in that war here on the home front an impressive new memorial designed by two San Francisco artists, Cheryl Barton and Susan Schwartzenberg.[8]

I was named by both the city of Richmond and the office of Assembly member Dion Aroner, for whom I worked as an aide, to be their representative on the planning team for the park. The second planning session I participated in was in the fall of 2003.

There were perhaps 35 to 40 experts in the room: marine engineers, city planners, architects, historians, developers, National Park Service staff, writers, scientists, and me. My name tag did not say *field representative* nor *city liaison*, nor did it honor the fact that I represented the State of California, which holds liens on much of the land that lies beneath the historic Ford assembly plant, an important component of the new national park. My name tag said simply, *"Former Rosie."*[9] It was an innocent sin of omission. I was aware that in this younger group, I was serving as a kind of icon of an era and valued for my "historic" value. But I was not to be allowed peer status. And, yes, I brought their attention to this oversight when the proper moment came.

I learned during this early planning session how history becomes revisionist.

In the new plan before us that day, the planning team was taken on a bus tour of the buildings that would be restored as elements in the park. They were on scattered sites throughout the western part of the city.

---

8   *EDITOR'S NOTE:* San Francisco–based Cheryl Barton is an internationally famous American landscape architect. Susan Schwartzenberg is a senior artist at San Francisco's Exploratorium museum.

9   And, of course, I never was a "Rosie" during the war in the first place, but rather a file clerk in the black auxiliary of a segregated labor union.

We saw, for example, one of the wartime housing complexes that had been preserved, Nystrom Village, which consists of modest bungalows, mostly duplexes and triplexes. These had been constructed "for white workers only." In many cases, the descendants of those workers still inhabited those homes. They're now historic landmarks and on the national registry as such.

But at the war's end, almost all of the structures that were set aside for African Americans—housing, recreation, and the old union hall—were razed to the ground in a vain attempt to get the black workers to leave Richmond and return to the Southern lands from which they had come.

Since we were "telling the story of America through structures," I wondered, *How in the world do we tell this one?* And in looking around the room that day, I realized that it was only a question for me. It held no meaning for anyone else.

No one else in the room realized that the story of Rosie the Riveter is a *white* woman's story. I and other women of color were not to be represented by this park as it was proposed. Many of the sites named in the enabling legislation I remembered as places of racial segregation and, as such, they might now end up being enshrined by a generation that had forgotten that history. It was then it first occurred to me that what gets remembered is a function of who is in the room doing the remembering. There was no one in that room with any reason to remember the segregation and racism of those times.

There is no way to explain the continuing presence of the 40 percent African American population in the city of Richmond's current residents without including their role in World War II. There continues to be a *custodial* attitude toward this segment of the population, with outsiders unaware of the miracle of those folks who dropped their hoes in the fields of those Southern states and came west. After only two weeks of training, they picked up welding torches to help save the world from the enemy. Even their grandchildren have lost the sense of mission and worthiness without those markers of achievement and "membership" in the greatest effort to save the world from Fascist domination.

And, yes, I did tell the park planners all of that at this session. At the time, I had no idea what they would do with the information, but I did feel a sense of having communicated those thoughts effectively to well-meaning professionals who didn't know what in hell to do with the information.

I was a Rosie who never saw a ship during that time. The little union hall that I had worked in as a young file clerk has long since been destroyed. It was far enough away from the shipyards to have gotten lost over time as memories dimmed. My memory had either censored all relationship to the period, or I never felt a part of the war effort at all. I did not arrive in the West at the start of the war. Having grown up in the Bay Area, I was an anomaly. I realize now that—at the time—I wasn't always sure just who the enemy was.

I was a part of the story now being told, though, and I was determined to do everything that I could to restore the missing chapters. But in those early days of the development of the park, the challenge was daunting, indeed.

IN LATE JUNE OF 2004, the call came to finalize my position with the National Park Service.

My answering machine spoke its message: "Betty, would you stop by sometime today to drop off your résumé? And, you'll need to include your academic stuff." Over the early months of the planning process for the park, I'd begun to act as a volunteer/consultant with the National Park Service, with primary responsibility still invested in my work for the California State Assembly. My work life had begun to morph into a period of transition without intent. Since I often met with National Park Service people while representing Assembly member Loni Hancock, this one had to be a slam dunk, right? Nope. Not so.

I stopped by the temporary park office with my neatly typed résumé in hand and presented it to Deputy Superintendent Rick Smith, the director of the Rosie the Riveter project. "We're bringing you in with a park ranger classification, Betty," he told me. That, apparently, had some criteria that my résumé—impressive though it may be—just doesn't have. Rick scanned the four-pager with all its interesting accomplishments and achievements, then asked for my academic credits. (Gulp!)

Since I'd married at 20 and spent the next 25 years raising a family of four kids, there had never been time for formal study. But I'd experienced more of life than most and learned from every new challenge. If they wanted to hire me, I told one of my children, Rick Smith would just have to convince his personnel department that I was a one-of-a-kind-talent-who-can't-be-quantified-or-measured-by-ordinary standards! Crazy? Sure, but that about summed it up. The poor man then asked for the name of my high school so he could secure whatever records were still there. (Got those little boxes to fill in, *donchaknow.*) Weird? Right. Let's see, that would be about 62 years ago. How relevant would such records be? The bureaucracy is such a slave to those little boxes, isn't it?

Rick had apparently set aside the fact that he'd been working with me for about three years, during which time we'd sat together in meetings with historians, engineers, park rangers, architects, politicians, museum directors, etc., in planning operations for the new national park. The reason they'd offered to me, specifically, the position of ranger at this newly created park in Richmond was because they'd obviously been impressed by the quality of my participation in their projects, right? Otherwise . . . ? Wassup?

But it appeared that they had to confer and get back to me after they'd received my Castlemont High School transcript.

Meanwhile, I'd had time to reread my résumé and found it a pretty good sketch of where my "professional life" had taken me, with or without advanced degrees. Had never felt more ready for next steps in a new direction. Being a park ranger was a little far-fetched, but what the hey . . . !

THE FIRST PHASE OF my work with the National Park Service ended at the end of September 2004. After I completed my 60-day assignment, it ended appropriately enough at a luncheon at the newly revived Port of Richmond—the home of Kaiser Shipyard Number Three—at which auto warehousers from Korea entertained Bay Area officials and members of the industry along with park personnel. The elaborate luncheon for about 200 dignitaries was simulcast to the home port in Spokane, and videoconferenced to other sites. Huge social event, and the introduction of this new industrial enterprise to the world.

I had spent lots of time during my Park Service work being quietly enraged to discover that, though credited with advancing racial integration by many years through his hiring policies at the shipyards, it is also true that Henry J. Kaiser brought racial segregation to the West Coast in all its ugliness. By bringing the races together in Richmond's shipyards, however, Kaiser may well have accelerated the move toward racial equality by a good many years, if only as an unintended consequence of those policies.

Kaiser's major recruitment efforts were in the five Southern States of Texas, Oklahoma, Arkansas, Mississippi, and Louisiana. His workforce was made up primarily of poor whites coming up from the Dust Bowl, blacks fleeing from the slow mechanization of cotton production, and all of those just recovering from the great depression of the '30s.

Only a man with the audacity of Henry Kaiser would dare to bring into a town with a population of 23,000 a workforce of 98,000 black and white Southerners who wouldn't be sharing drinking fountains or any kind of public accommodations for another 20 years back in the states they had come from. There would be no time for focus groups or diversity training. They were all living under the threat of Fascist world domination, and there was no time to take on a broken social system. They would have to negotiate at the individual level every hour of every day in order to complete the mission of their leader, which was to build ships faster than the enemy could sink 'em in order to save the world.

Kaiser and his workforce of sharecroppers did their part by building 747 ships in three years and eight months, working on three shifts a day for 364 days a year with only Christmas off.[10] Henry Kaiser had never built a ship, but by introducing the prefab-

---

10   *EDITOR'S NOTE:* By way of comparison, Moore's Dry Dock in Oakland—a traditional shipbuilder since World War I—completed 100 ships in that same period, and at Marinship in Sausalito, Bechtel Corporation completed 93.

rication techniques Ford was using in auto manufacturing, he revolutionized shipbuilding. And by outproducing the enemy using these techniques, Kaiser and his workers helped to turn the tide of the war and bring World War II to an end in 1945.

I discovered that, though the shipyards introduced the concept of 24-hour day care for Kaiser's workers, which enabled Rosies to enter the workforce, it is also true that those facilities were not open to African American families.

There had been some recognition by the government in the middle of World War II of the need to reward the African American war workers in some significant ways. The Tuskegee Airmen, the Pearl Harbor naval hero Dorie Miller, and the heroic tank division that fought so valiantly in southern Europe with General George Patton had earned an indisputable place in the lore of the country. In response, there were 17 Liberty ships named for famous black citizens. Four that were built and launched to great celebrations here in Richmond were the SS *George Washington Carver*, the SS *Robert S. Abbott* (named for the publisher of the African American *Chicago Defender* newspaper), the SS *John Hope* (named for the noted black educator), and the SS *Harriet Tubman*. In addition, there were five Victory ships named for historically black colleges: the SS *Fisk Victory*, the SS *Xavier Victory*, the SS *Talladega*, the SS *Lane Victory*, and the SS *Tuskegee Victory*.

By far the most intriguing finds I uncovered in the log of ships launched in Richmond in March and April of 1944 were the SS *Ethiopia Victory* and the SS *Toussaint L'Ouverture*, the latter a Liberty ship named for the great black revolutionary leader who led Haitians against the French in the early 1800s. What I wouldn't give to be able to unearth records of the discussions that led to these choices! When we recall that these honors were conferred at a time when segregation was still full-blown and when the country was still locked in the grip of Jim Crow, it seems miraculous that—even then—there were those who were trying desperately to "get it right." And there still are.

This suggested an important rationale for the teaching of black history to African American children. Embedded in such teachings is the invisible pride builder of self-respect. *"We, too, have heroes, and I, too, can be one"* comes from knowing what's gone before. I learned as a small-business owner in Berkeley—in a very low-income community—*that people learn to respect only by being respected*, and that it is rarely otherwise.

During that summer of 2004 in Richmond, we reeled from the senseless killing of a 17-year-old African American standout student and athlete, Terrance Kelly. He was only a day away from escaping a questionable future in a crime-ridden corner of the community. He'd received an athletic scholarship and was leaving for Oregon to enter college. The only defense of the 16-year-old youngster who wielded the gun that ended Terrance's life was that he'd been *"dissed"* (i.e., disrespected). I'm not sure that any of us were aware at the time of just how important that word had become in communities where—since slavery, Jim Crow, and the struggles for equality in this city following WWII—there has been so little respect to draw upon.

Due to inadequate education from revisionist textbooks that left out all references to meaningful black history until recent years, and despite the efforts of a few enlightened teachers, the lack thereof may have become lethal in some frightening way. *Dissing* is the word used by youth, but the feeling expressed by the word is universally recognizable, a feeling that crosses the generations and robs us all of some immutable something that we can rarely define, that by now is buried deep in the DNA of our children, that bleeds out of our pores, restricts our vision, and profoundly limits opportunities to gain and live a lifestyle worthy of achieving it.

My work with the National Park Service had ended far too soon. I was just getting into the rhythm of it. My original four-year contract had come to an end. Now I was seriously considering ways to get the City of Richmond to engage me to oversee a year-long centennial celebration. Far-fetched? Of course it was. They had no idea that they even needed one, or that they needed me to give it life. As has been true many times in the past, I was running around with answers to questions that nobody was asking!

But the park found other work for me to do. I'd originally been hired on a four-year contract that was ending soon. I would eventually become an interpretive park ranger with permanent status. In the summer of 2005 I found myself working, with a different job title than before, with a lovely young ranger, Naomi Torres, who came as a transfer from the Golden Gate National Recreation Area at the Presidio across the bay and was brought on board as our chief of interpretation. Together, Naomi and I would be planning the outreach strategies that would bring together the local communities with the Rosie the Riveter/WWII Home Front National Historical Park. She was scheduled to be working with me only two days a week, and otherwise I supposed that I would be on my own.

I'D NEVER ANTICIPATED NEEDING to explain the origins of my blog, since this was always a conversation I was having with *myself*, and therefore it never needed explanation. In the beginning, the only intended audience was my children and theirs, and those yet unborn, and I'm not even certain that I'd ever thought to inform them of its existence, or that anyone beyond the family would have any interest in its contents.

I started writing my blog in the fall of 2003, but its origins go well before that.

Back in the late '90s, I'd been working on my family history for months through visits to the Mormon Oakland California FamilySearch Library and to the genealogy websites then developing online. It slowly began to dawn on me that the women got lost entirely in these histories or were nearly impossible to follow. It was frustrating when an interesting ancestor would unceremoniously drop out of sight as a name changed through marriage, or simply cease to exist in the records due to changed and unexplained relationships. Though there were obviously many colorful and fascinating women down through the ages, people I hungered to know more about, everything rested with the males in the lineage.

I'd lived through some tumultuous history during my lifetime, and how an *ordinary* woman survived those times surely should have been as fascinating to those unknown future historians as it would have been for me to be able to know how our ancestors got through those perilous periods of slavery and reconstruction, yet survived to produce my generation. It felt as if a debt might be owed to those who had preceded me in life, a debt that I could assume because *I*, and my generation, were that legacy that their pain and suffering made possible.

Those years of research had changed unalterably my perceptions of my own place in history and the world, and given me a strong sense of the continuity of Life.

At some point there arose a need to leave footprints of my own life for the family historians of the future to follow. *I* would not be lost. The experience of reconstructing our family history had given me a deep sense of having a foundation upon which to build, and that those few bricks I was contributing to that family foundation would help to erect the platform upon which the next generation of our young women would stand.

Owning my first computer opened up possibilities undreamed of, but—as I was untrained in the field—that first post in September of 2003 was just a stab at finding a place to stand while I figured out the parameters and how to "make it up as it went along."

I had little sense of anyone actually reading it. I didn't dream of the possibility of an unseen and unrelated readership having any interest in its contents.

Blog entry, Saturday, September 3, 2005

I wrote these words in the immediate aftermath of the horror of the hurricane called Katrina and the bursting of the dikes that had protected my New Orleans from the raging Mississippi, and as I watched it all unfold, evening after evening, on my television. Fortunately, as bad as Katrina and its aftermath came to be, many of the things I had feared at the time about family and place did not.

I am aware of having dropped some invisible internal control button to "dim" so that the horrendous pain of the loss of an entire culture is now occurring both inside and outside of me . . . maybe Creole-Cajun life and history really does die with my generation.

The human loss is beyond comprehension. If I hear one more commentator give the body count as "147" right behind the mentions of "bodies floating by, being abandoned in attics, left by the sides of roads and in Superdome restrooms," I'll scream! After all, those uncounted bodies of the weak, of the too young or too old or too black, have been floating by now for almost a week! There are reports of rats being seen claiming the remains. The body count in the city of my ancestry and early childhood will surely rise to thousands in days to come.

Spent most of the past several days searching the web's survivor lists for cousins I can scarcely remember but feel deeply connected to by our common ancestry. They're so alive for me due to the countless hours spent in reconstructing that history, from the 1500s to the present. That history is gathered into two huge binders and on the walls of vintage photos that line the hallway of my apartment. Perhaps what I've collected over the years will become the family archives and the only record of this family's long tenure in the country and the world. Ours is the story of black America with all of its pain, anguish, and glory. *Up From Slavery* is a book title that I recall from my early years. Can't recall the author at the moment, but what it describes in those few words speaks volumes about where life's journey has taken the Allen/Charbonnet/Breaux clan. Katrina may have erased that record of our existence.

Not only are those ancestors so alive for me still, but the structures left by the builders of my family—my grandfather, Louis Charbonnet; my dad, Dorson Louis Charbonnet; and his seven brothers. Corpus Christi Catholic Church, the rice mill, the high school in the

Tremé, all designed and built by my grandfather and his sons many years ago, and that I visited from California as a teen *to discover it racially segregated with white New Orleanians occupying the middle pews and people who looked like me sitting on both sides*. It's surely gone now in the rage of a hurricane called Katrina. Its segregated history reduces its value to me not one iota. It is the system that *was*, and that may have exemplified for us a low point in our collective lives that may now be overcome because we've experienced another soul-shaking exposure of our sins. Maybe we can move now toward redemption.

Then there were our family homes on Lapeyrouse, Frenchmen, and Touro Streets, and the Convent of the Holy Family Sisters out on Gentilly. My second husband, Bill, and I visited that Charbonnet-designed and -constructed institution the year before he died. I remember now running my hand across the cornerstone bearing my grandfather's name and the dates hoping to remember the physical impression well enough to bring those impressions back *alive* to my blind father upon returning to the Bay Area. This was the convent that housed the first African American nuns in the nation, the Holy Family Sisters, an order dedicated to the care and education of black children at a time when there was little else to turn to. Surely it no longer stands since it was built not far from the lake. It is my guess that those good sisters may well have remained in place as the water rose. They may have perished in service to their people and to "The Lord." The Order was still very much together when we visited, complete with the little draped window near the heavily secured front doors, through which frightened young girls could slip blanketed newborns without blame or guilt, to be raised by the nuns or placed out in the parish for adoption.

Most of my family's dead are entombed in aboveground crypts in St. Louis cemetery on the edge of St. Louis Cathedral in the Tremé. The tears come as I wonder whether their graves—some that date from the early 1800s—still exist . . . ? The French Quarter may have held. I don't really know.

My cousin, former Louisiana state representative Louis Charbonnet III, and his family have been evacuated to Baton Rouge. Other family members have been evacuated to Wisconsin, Florida, Texas, and St. Louis. Cousin Louis's legislative district included the French Quarter. His family's mortuary, Charbonnet-Labat-Glapion—which featured jazz funerals and red-bean feeds in its parking lot on Mardi Gras Day—was an important cultural landmark in the city they so loved. It surely was destroyed by Katrina.

But what is the most disturbing is that in the course of my work—where I'm working hard to help to expand the WWII story to include that of African Americans—I'm experiencing newly activated anger at racial segregation and economic deprivation. Watching the horrific images being spat out nonstop from our television screens by what appears to be a newly aware press corps revives mind pictures of slavery, lynchings, Selma, fire hoses, attack dogs, etc. The only comfort I can find is in the growing conviction that the numbers of outraged citizens of all colors, sizes, and social and economic levels has grown exponentially and that this may usher in, finally, a time of reconciliation.

I find hope in the fact that newsmen and -women on the spot were suddenly seeing new awful truths and awakening to what so many of us who've lived the history have always known: that the nation is deeply divided and must ultimately come to terms with its shameful history in order to finally move toward love and compassion that crosses barriers of race, gender, and privilege. Perhaps in the days to come, they will be able to reflect this in reports on the most powerful system of communication the world has ever known. Maybe they can hurry the healing before it's too late . . .

Do you suppose there is any possibility that this sick country can take a page from President Nelson Mandela's book—with the help of our newly awakened media—and create a Truth Commission and seek reconciliation?

But then, the phenomenon of Katrina heralds a new age, one in which nature's awesome power will continue to bring the world to its knees because the greed of man blinded him to the warnings of global warming before it was too late . . .

And in that knowing place deep within, I, quietly—no longer envy the young.

Unless we manage to outlive or out-gun those currently in the seats of power in this nation. I no longer rule out the possibility of armed revolution, something I could never imagine in my worst nightmares. Almost anything is possible in these times of such horrendous loss of our institutional underpinnings . . .

. . . And we're the *"Leaders of the Free World!"*

I'D BEEN WANDERING AROUND in the past during the last weeks of the summer of 2005. Started with Katrina and with my concern about the possible loss of kinfolk and a culture that I should have forgotten long ago but hadn't. Those ties of family and culture are obviously unbreakable as long as one's memories withstand the ravages of time.

But that was all in the background of my life. It was the *foreground* that was so commanding those summer days. The 60-day emergency hire under which the National Park Service had brought me in was due to expire on September 30. But in the interim, a new park superintendent had been brought in, a new phase of the work of park development had commenced, and the work of liaison between the park and the community had moved into sharper focus. They'd also found funding to keep me into some indefinite future. It was open-ended, but then so am I, right? I was due to be hired as a full-fledged national park staffer when my contract ended. Maybe my classification would be "Living Artifact." Maybe folks would be required to wear those little museum white gloves in order to shake my hand. Didn't know. But it felt good.

Age had brought with it a new confidence that continued to amaze even me. It was only since I had reached 80 that I was able to say with assurance, "I *know!*" No longer did I wait around for some avatar to deliver me or those who trust me for answers that I no longer expect to find, or that don't exist and never did, or were unattainable over the course of any single lifetime. I not only *knew*, but was willing to act on the *knowing*. This didn't imply, however, that I was necessarily correct in what I knew, just that I'd become quite comfortable with conflicting truths and could now live nicely with ambiguity.

The archives and the library just outside my cubicle held theses, photographs, artifacts, slides, posters of the period, oral histories, recently written books by historians who were only then discovering the period. After all, 60 years isn't a great enough time span to invite much scholarly investigation as *history*. Those 60 years, however, represented the lion's share of my life at the time, but apparently not the most productive years.

The ones remaining to be lived might be the most productive yet.

Ain't that a hoot?

ONE NIGHT IN THE summer of 2006, several of us met at the Nevin Community Center in the Iron Triangle district of Richmond with the residents of the neighborhood that lies within what is now designated the Rosie the Riveter/WWII Home Front National Historical Park for a presentation by the firm that is doing the design for a complete new streetscape for the abandoned historic downtown district of the city of Richmond. For the past several years—as a field rep for Assemblywomen Dion Aroner and, later, Loni Hancock—I'd participated as a member of a number of advisory groups that contributed to where we were that summer. We were engaged in the process of restoring the abandoned central core of the city. When completed, the full length of this main street would be reconfigured, reconstructed, and restored to its former glory as the primary artery through the city. It runs from the Santa Fe–Baltimore & Ohio railroad yards in the west to San Pablo Avenue on the east. This was a *major* undertaking.

Having served on the advisory committee to the design team that redesigned the entire district (Old Town, Civic Center, and beyond), my relationship to the project was almost constant from the beginning, but there was a difference now. My role had changed—maybe deepened—in that the relationship to the project now involved the city of Richmond's new role as a *host city* to a brand-new national park, and I was *now* employed by the National Park Service to work with others as the community outreach staffer to bring the city and the federal agency together in the creation of the park.

Since joining the National Park Service staff a year before, I'd concentrated on raising public awareness of the fact that the previously abandoned inner core of this beleaguered city was now the central piece in the park that was slated to become a *world* destination. The park consisted not only of the four shoreline Kaiser shipyards, the SS *Red Oak Victory* (the last surviving ship built therein), the beautiful Albert Kahn–designed Ford Assembly Plant, but, in addition, about 20 war-related structures scattered throughout the historic old downtown area and along the scenic shoreline. In this respect, it was a unique park that required new sensibilities.

In most places where national parks are located, the properties on which they sit are owned by the Park Service through the Department of the Interior. Here in Richmond, the structures were either owned by individuals or in commercial or nonprofit hands or otherwise out of the public domain. For instance, the old 23rd Street Greyhound bus station was now a Mexican-Peruvian restaurant that we hoped could be marked with a plaque that described the role it played during the war years in bringing so many strangers here. Sidewalks might have landmarking plaques embedded where many relevant places, now gone, once stood.

Kaiser walked away at war's end, leaving behind a city that had grown from 23,000 to 130,000. Then, it was a bustling wartime city with nine movie theaters and major department stores, but it became an economic ghost town over time, with much of the postwar redevelopment taking place at the city's outer edges and away from its inner core, leaving behind jobless, homeless, deserted people who'd been brought west a short time before to fill the ranks of home front workers who built the ships and helped to defeat the enemy in a time of national need.

Over the year I had worked with the park so far, I became aware of a relatively new concept that had been adopted by the National Park Service, that of "civic engagement." This meant that there was a mandate from the top that new ways be found to build a stronger relationship between *communities* and *places* that we hold as worthy of reverence and/or through which we share *history in common* as a nation. Richmond, by an act of Congress five years earlier, was designated such a place. We had only to grow the awareness of that fact with a community that had suffered slow degradation over the past 60 or more years. Many of the structures now marked for reverence existed only through benign neglect and had been awaiting the wrecking ball for decades. The only factor that saved them was undoubtedly the lack of funds with which to do the work. In more affluent cities, war-related sites have been slowly disappearing, being replaced by sports stadia, industrial parks, etc. Richmond was on a slower time schedule, I suppose, and not particularly reverent about its past.

There was much to be learned from the people of this city, and I believed the park might help to reveal that to the nation and the world. Only problem was that I didn't think the city was aware of its uniqueness yet. My work involved finding ways to reveal this reality to those who were currently living it, as well as to those who would come to revere these heroic workers and sites and structures that served as background for the women and minorities who came here to serve in the home front mobilization that helped to save the world.

OVER A WEEKEND LATE in the summer of 2007, I got to test my ability to adapt to the demands of being, like comic Kathy Griffin, a "D-list celebrity." It was a mixed blessing. On the one hand, I fully enjoyed the new respect being shown for the National Park Service and for my role in it. The wearing of the uniform took some getting used to, since hardly anyone was as impressed by it as *I* was. Truly. I was in awe of it, and reasoned that I would probably have to watch myself closely for signs of arrogance in the days to come. I felt at least six inches taller, and it was never more apparent than when I was acting as a tour guide with my ranger partner.

Before I was uniformed, properly hatted, and badged, I sat quietly in one of the seats on the bus somewhere near the middle, believing that the most important part of my work had already been completed in the managing of the logistics of the bus tour: taking the reservations, keeping the roster and doing the confirmations, seeing to it that the physical arrangements were properly completed, etc. That was enough. But that had changed rather dramatically.

Since becoming an *authentic* tour guide, I now stood proudly behind the driver. My co-guide still carried the lion's share of the narration, but now I was actively adding to the presentation, filling in the blanks, sharing my own stories of the period, being careful to include any and all references to the racial segregation effects extant during those years. I was discovering that there were a lot more words under my ranger's hat than I'd ever have guessed!

I was fast becoming a kind of "authority" on the period, and was finding it easy to do that presentation *factually* and with little anger or emotion. It had the flavor of a *performance*, so to speak. That history simply *was*. I'd arrived at these advanced years with a sense of moral rightness on my side and with little need to blame. *Truth* makes its own statement, and I could *see* people "getting it." What an *amazing* experience . . .

Besides that, I may have outlived all those folks whose memory differed from mine!

That summer weekend I was invited to attend the centennial celebration of San Pablo Park in Berkeley, where I'd spent so many of my earlier years, both with my grandfather, Papa George, and with that large and rich Bay Area black community that made the park their weekend gathering point in the years before the war.

I'd asked permission from my supervisor to treat my attendance at the ceremonies as an official event and attended in full park ranger uniform. But once there, I felt overdressed. I realized that my honoring of the memory of friends and family and mentors during my many years visiting San Pablo Park was a private thing. I had no reason or need to impress anyone by the wearing of a uniform. The only saving grace was that there were hundreds of children there, and seeing little girls glance at me admiringly held its own magic. It helped me become aware that each time I was in a public situation, I silently "announced" the opening of a new career path to those children who had never seen a park ranger of color in uniform, and that was a powerful message to send.

Blog Entry, Wednesday, March 12, 2008

It never dawned—while filing change-of-address cards or taking dues payments in the small office of the racially segregated Boilermakers A-36 union hall—that I might live long enough to actually *become* black history, but so it seems. Despite a fading memory of working in that unassuming little office located somewhere on Barrett Avenue in Richmond, and a reluctance to identify as the proverbial "Rosie the Riveter," life has placed a soapbox under my feet and I'm speaking publicly for a generation for whom my presence in the workforce was questionable at best.

As one of the diminishing female home front workers of World War II still standing, I often feel undeserving of the "Rosie" title. I'm increasingly called upon to speak for a generation that helped to save the world from Nazi imperialism, but often feel that I'm fulfilling that role by default since so many of those voices have been silenced by time. And since the equality for which *we* worked, fought, and died has yet to be fully realized.

Time tends to soften, alter, and revise history, and the home front stories of WWII are no exception. During those years, I was a 20-year-old politically naïve woman of color with little understanding of the war except for the disruption it brought to everyday life. Confusion reigned as if a major fault line had shifted under the weight of the unprecedented population explosion that changed the social fabric of the Bay Area, the West Coast, and the nation.

The confusion was driven by still-raw memories of a nation that, in 1941, assigned 91 percent of black women to work in a few categories: agricultural, household, and industrial service jobs. Performing clerical work in a segregated union hall—menial though it might be in the scheme of things—was a step up from making beds, caring for children, emptying bedpans in hospitals, and mopping floors for white Americans.

Yet, in the wake of having become a full-time park ranger for the National Park Service, I find myself invited to speak for that generation, to share the stories of the times to groups large and small.

Does it feel real? Have I learned to accept my role as spokesperson for a period in history that holds painful and often humiliating memories? Oddly enough, the answer is yes. I find that today's audiences are ready to explore the WWII era with an openness that holds the potential for promoting a continuing movement toward positive social change. This might well ensure that my granddaughter's generation will benefit from my participation in this long-overdue national conversation.

The silence that worked against change has given way to new possibilities for measuring progress toward a more equitable society, and Rosie the Riveter World War II Home Front National Historical Park is in a position to accelerate that movement through the "Lost Conversations and Untold Stories" that I'm able to provide in this new public role.

Perhaps the trajectory of my life from a young and confused file clerk to a full-time national park ranger on a soapbox illustrates as much as today's campaigns for the presidency—a woman and an African American—just how far we've come in the ongoing process of growing our imperfect democracy to the benefit of the world.

JULY 2009 brought the 65th anniversary of the Port Chicago disaster that took 320 lives, 202 of whom were young African Americans. I had the great honor of providing a tour of the Rosie the Riveter Memorial Park for a group of men (the "mutineers") who survived that tragedy and returned for that year's commemoration.[11]

Prior to arriving to meet me for the tour, they'd traveled in a caravan consisting of two large vans and a sedan to the national cemetery at San Bruno on the San Francisco Peninsula, where they'd visited the graves of those who perished in that conflagration on July 17, 1944. I learned during the ceremony a fact long forgotten: *Their* graves are separated from the others by race. At that time, no servicemen of color were buried with the whites, instead being segregated into a section "for colored only," and this was not in some *Southern* graveyard, but here in California, where such practices were little known. Of course, this would have happened before the desegregation of the armed forces, so it would not have been questioned at the time. What a cruel irony to revisit! We have so much still to atone for as a nation, don't we? As I've said before, if others will continue to work on atonement, we'll continue to strive valiantly to find forgiveness.

I went online and looked at the inscription that's at the Golden Gate National Cemetery site and saw that in the graphic on the website, it talks about the general who's buried there, the other people who were buried there. It gives a couple of sentences to the Italian and German prisoners of war who died in captivity, who

---

11   *EDITOR'S NOTE:* Within a month following the July 17, 1944, munitions explosion that killed 320 sailors, 202 of them African American, the Navy resumed munitions-unloading operations at a nearby site under similarly unsafe conditions. More than 200 African American sailors refused to unload munitions until the unsafe conditions were cured. Fifty of them were charged and convicted as mutineers.

were also buried there. And then, as an afterthought, it mentions that also buried in this cemetery, in the colored section, are the 22 caskets buried as "unknowns," without mentioning that there were 320 who died, without mentioning an explosion, without mentioning that they were even sailors.

On the first day of the Port Chicago remembrance at the memorial site I had attended when I became a park ranger some years before, I remembered seeing that the first two rows had signs on them saying they were reserved for the survivors of Port Chicago. And there were only two, I think, African Americans in those seats as they began to file in. And I didn't understand why, because by then I had at least become familiar with the Port Chicago story. And why were there not more survivors? When the keynote speaker was gone and people began to jump up to talk about their experiences during the explosion, I learned the answer. They were all survivors of the *town* of Port Chicago. They were all white town folks.

So their memories were of being in the theater, of being in bed, having their walls collapse and their windows blown out. And I suddenly realized that what was being remembered was dependent upon who was doing the remembering, and that history doesn't necessarily do a disservice to African American memory as much as it is dependent upon *who's in the room*. And that in time, who was in the room was going to be dominated by the no-longer-existent town of Port Chicago, and that the African American story—even though there were 202 men lost—was going to simply be covered over, not by design, but by circumstance. Those African American sailors who were on the loading docks and in the ships that went down in the explosion were too young to have left survivors. And that the fact that they had been mere boys at the time of the explosion—not men—was key. They would not have fathered children. And so it was terribly important that as a participant in the creation of this park, if it was going to be a park—because at that time, the Port Chicago memorial was only a monument—I needed to be a surrogate survivor, because that history was dependent upon people like me remembering. And that's often how history happens. It's not that people don't want to remember, it's that circumstances crowd out truth.

That is, unless we can revive the history of those men and what they went through, because of their unintended gift to us, which was that the explosion and the mutiny that followed, and the public response to the unfairness of the deaths of those who died, and the trial of those who resisted—were the trigger that caused President Truman to desegregate the armed forces. That the role they played, even by being destroyed, fed into the desegregation of the armed forces, which subsequently led into the entire dismantling of the system of segregation throughout the country.

Port Chicago played a pivotal role in that I think it triggered the modern Civil Rights Movement, which, I think, began with the response to Port Chicago, because that's where African Americans said we will not be backed up any further than this. That's where people began to not accept the status quo.

And I'm just convinced that those men's lives were not wasted, that they were sacrificed, but they were not wasted, that they really did trumpet and dictate the next 20 years of social change. That is what Port Chicago means to me.

BY THE SPRING OF 2011, we had become a four-park consortium that included Port Chicago at the Naval Weapons Station in Concord, the Eugene O'Neill National Historic Site in Danville, the John Muir National Historic Site in Martinez, and our own Rosie the Riveter Park in Richmond. Rosie the Riveter had enjoyed a tripling of staff at all levels, and was expecting still more. All of the new staff members were seasoned in their fields, having gained their earlier experience at other parks in the system. Many came from the wilderness parks and were having their first urban park experience and learning the lore, the history of their new assignments. They brought newness and enthusiasm and a curiosity to the work that enlivened our days and challenged stereotypes.

But I was having a persistent need to disassociate myself from the "Rosie the Riveter" story. I'd always considered that story a part of the myth of the emancipation of women into the workforce, and my contention had always been that this did not apply to women of color. We'd been working outside the home since slavery given the fact that, until recent times, black men had been limited to the lowest-paying service-sector jobs, so it had always taken two salaries to support black families. My WWII job for Boilermakers A-36, a Jim Crow union created for blacks, only meant that I had never seen myself as the romantic Rosie of "We can do it" fame.

I had become increasingly uncomfortable with my position. It wasn't that I felt it was untrue or unjustified, it's just that there was a legitimate white Rosie story that wasn't being told and that needed to be, and that white women needed to be demanding more from that history than a catchy tune, red bandannas, posters, and belated kudos.

WWII did not bring American women into the workplace for the first time. That's a myth. Women have been working since time immemorial, only it was not called "work" until we were introduced to what had formerly been male occupations. What women did was always defined as our life roles: to be ever in support of the men of the society. We have always been secretaries, librarians, teachers, nurses, and always supportive of men, with few exceptions. Women's work consisting of child care, general housekeeping, shopping, washing and ironing, budgeting, or preparing meals was considered "what wives do" until we were recruited during the war into the workforce to do welding, riveting, conducting orchestras, dispatching trucks, engineering, reading blueprints, ferrying aircraft into war zones, contracting, manufacturing munitions, assembling jeeps and tanks—all work—for the first time in history.

Despite the fact that Rosie was often a poor woman whose opportunities were limited before she entered the defense industry, the romanticized vision that endures was that she was a middle-class white woman (played by Katharine Hepburn or Rosalind Russell) who called her hairdresser or manicurist to cancel her next appointments and headed for the shipyards and aircraft plants to sign on as a replacement for our fighting men. That those pioneer women who were widowed by the Civil War and World

War I had not been workers—though they raised large families, alone, on farms they ran themselves.

In the tragic Triangle Shirtwaist Factory fire of 1911 in which 149 lives were lost, immigrant women working for as little as $6 a week under such conditions that in the aftermath, the horrific conditions of the workplaces in the garment industry came under harsh scrutiny, and the movement for unionization was strengthened. Were those women of 1911 not workers? Were those migrant sweatshop workers even counted as women?

Maybe, in time, some powerful, gutsy white feminist whose passion for her story equals mine for my black story will appear out of the blue to guide walking tours at that great Rosie the Riveter Memorial on the Richmond marina and make the feminist story come alive. And maybe we'll get around to processing the Civil War before I trade my ranger flat-hat for a French beret!

But leaning against the wall of the theater in the park visitor center watching a showing of the short documentary film *Untold Stories*,[12] trying to be as inconspicuous as possible, it dawned on me the effect this newly created national park was having on this city. The insistence upon total honesty as we revisit the era of what is remembered as "The Good War" had proven to be unquestionably wise.

Rosie the Riveter/WWII Home Front National Historical Park was providing the narrative of the "great mobilization," the coming together of people from Everywhere, USA, in response to a world-threatening international crisis. Those years saw the creation of the cauldron into which the nation's conflicting social mores and patterns were cast, resulting in two decades of life-changing chaos out of which the causes of civil and human rights were painfully carved, bringing us more in line with the promises of our founding documents and loudly professed but sorrowfully unfulfilled national ideals.

---

12   *EDITOR'S NOTE: Of Lost Conversations and Untold Stories* was a four-minute video written and narrated by Betty Soskin that described the African American experience in Richmond during the World War II years.

Since 1776, we've been a revolutionary country painfully at odds with a set of core principles and values for which we've been willing for generations to fight and die, but *by which we've miserably failed to live.* We've deceived the world by holding out a tempting imaginary chalice of peace and freedom while holding to contradictions and an arrogance that denied their ever entering into our reality. The WWII home front mobilization and subsequent struggles for redefinition forced us to move through to a more honest alignment with those core beliefs. But as a nation of diverse ordinary people in transition, it all happened with mind-numbing speed, *far* too rapidly for us to process.

It is *that* story that *Richmond* tells. Those years (1941 to 1964 and beyond) forced us to reexamine the relationships between human and civil rights and even the possibility of a world at peace. Without the insistent stress upon the everyday lives of ordinary people living in extraordinary times, without the urgent demands of the war years to find ways to live and work together despite a nonsupportive and unforgiving social system, and without *their persistent and sometimes combative resistance to continuing to any longer endure the contradictions*, the nation might never have reached this place of transformation.

Untold Stories revealed the raw material from which the new understandings have been carved. Out of such sorrowful history world peace may yet be born. *I believe that the City of Richmond provided the background against which the country first began to confront its contradictions and correct its course—entering a period of 20 years of social upheaval, echoes of which still resonate from our nation's lecterns, pulpits, and town squares.* We're still a work in progress.

Perhaps Rosie was more than a mere riveter, but the ultimate symbol for change of a kind that we're only now beginning to fully understand and appreciate.

9

SHINING BRIGHT
AT TWILIGHT:
Lessons of a Life Long Lived

WHAT'S IN A NAME? Everything, I suppose, though I had no idea that the question held any meaning for me. It does.

Having been christened under my centuries-old surname of Charbonnet, I'd married Melvin Reid in 1942 and become Betty Reid. After having been married to Mel for over 35 years, we divorced and I met and married Dr. William F. Soskin, whose own name was actually changed from Sosinski at the insistence of two older sisters when Bill entered the University of Michigan. Ironically, at the time his sisters were seeking ways to avoid the bigotry being suffered by the Polish people in the Midwest, not realizing that they'd taken in its place a Jewish surname that would invite other bigotry.

Since I'd spent at least two decades as Betty *Reid* while living in the world of Northern California suburbia, I was clearly identified in that world under Mel's last name.

When we divorced I returned to Berkeley to take up life as a faculty wife in a totally new social setting where I was now known as Bill Soskin's Betty *Soskin*. I insisted upon carrying both my married names during our 10-year marriage since my children were all Reids, and it felt important for me to connect my name to theirs.

By this time I'd developed two separate identities: one as the wife of a well-known African American businessman who had been a stay-at-home suburban mother but had also become a political activist with significant "street cred" under her belt and a growing reputation as a poet/singer; and now the new identity as a faculty wife of a brilliant professor who was doing groundbreaking research for the University of California at Berkeley. Few in the university years had any knowledge of the former Betty Reid, who had been unceremoniously left in the all-white suburbs behind the East Bay hills.

But both these men—Mel and Bill—died in 1987 within a three-month period, and, since I'd allowed myself to be defined in relation to each, for several months after their deaths I wasn't sure just who I was now that they were gone.

For years afterward, I suppose that I was attempting to forge those identities into some kind of wholeness, with a certain amount of success.

But now there arises in me a wish to return to my original self, the girl who once bore the name *Charbonnet*, but who lost it to *custom*. My parents gave birth to three daughters, of whom I'm the only survivor. There were no sons to carry the name into the future. With me, our historic name dies, a name that traces back in this country to about 1768, to the 14th century in Europe. My two husbands both died decades ago, leaving me to fend for myself in an often unsympathetic world, but also returning the *me* of me to myself to do with as I wished, right? Right behind the grief stood emancipation, to be assumed when I was ready.

I RARELY AWAKEN SO tired, as if I'd been wrestling with demons throughout the night, and in a way, I suppose I had that night in the summer of 2005.

For the first time in a very long time Papa George had visited me in dreams, probably summoned by the Edgar Ray Killen verdict in Philadelphia, Mississippi—where the aging Klansman was found guilty in the lynching murders of three young civil rights workers in 1964[13]—plus my angst around the parade of United States senators who had refused to sign on to that recently introduced anti-lynching resolution.[14]

I remembered Papa's stories about how when he was a boy in rural Louisiana, he heard whispers about those luckless African Americans who'd been caught by the infamous Ku Klux Klan, and that the usual result of the chase would be that the victim would be hog-tied ankles to wrists behind the back, tossed into the back of a wagon or pickup truck, then set down at the edge of the levee on his knees. The murderers would jump on his back until his spine shattered. Only then would they toss him into the river to drown. It was chilling to the seven-year-old Betty, standing beside Papa George as we weeded the vegetable garden together. His younger brother—my great-uncle—Albert had fled as a young man to Kansas, never to return to St. James Parish. It was rumored that he'd shot and killed a Klansman in self-defense and was being hunted by the Night Riders. I don't believe that Papa ever saw him again. I'm not sure that he spoke much about Albert to anyone but me. I can still see that vacant place in his eyes—as though he were really alone and talking to himself—the way grown-ups do when they don't expect answers. Then he'd laugh and sing another of his crazy little song snatches to dismiss the agony of memory and bring us both back to the moment and the endless pulling of the weeds . . .

But the listening was terribly hard, and the nightmares that followed . . .

Those images came up again for me that night, all mixed in with the kids killing kids on Richmond's streets, and the three civil rights workers murdered in Mississippi 41 years before. I remembered that during the long search for those

---

13   *EDITOR'S NOTE:* Edgar Ray Killen was found guilty of three counts of manslaughter in June of 2005 for the murders of Student Nonviolent Coordinating Committee workers James Chaney, Andrew Goodman, and Michael Schwerner during the 1964 Freedom Summer black-voter registration drive in Mississippi.

14   In June of 2005, the United States Senate approved by voice vote a resolution apologizing for the Senate's failure to enact federal anti-lynching legislation in the 1890s, during the height of the lynching of African Americans throughout the South.

bodies, a number of black bodies were discovered when they dragged the various Mississippi rivers, bodies no one ever bothered to identify.

It was those deaths and Papa George's stories of the "black logs"—the bodies of murdered dark people—found in the Mississippi from time to time that created this song I once composed:

Black Log

black log driftin' down da bayou in de mawnin'
limbs a-draggin' 'gainst da willow
black log floatin' down da bayou in da mawnin'
now it's sun-up, Owl must leave you
time to fine his mossy pillow

bullfrog croakin' out his grievin' from dis strange lily pad
three-finga, twisted lily pad
noontime—comes da rivah 'roun' de levee
Boy heah fish' fo his suppa-time
caught one! . . . no, tain't nuthin' . . . but a black log
black log rushin' down da rivah in de evenin'
log cain't see da evenin'
caught!—now free . . . , log 'n me . . . in da rivah—no retrievin'
comes da sea now—here's da open sea now!

Freedom!

Too late . . .

IN THE SPRING of 2008, the SS *Red Oak Victory* was undergoing restoration at Shipyard Three in Richmond. It was the last ship built in the Kaiser shipyards. It was one of the 747 ships completed and launched by Henry J. Kaiser—a cement manufacturer who'd never built a ship before he got the federal contract in World

War II!—and his ragtag workforce of thousands of former share-cropping older men and women of every race, newly emancipated white women, underage boys, and many of the disabled. That remarkable feat was accomplished in just three years and eight months of WWII. If you're keeping score, that would be launching a ship almost every other day, a feat never equaled since that time. The record shows that one ship, the SS *Robert E. Peary*, was successfully completed and launched in four days, 15 hours, and 29 minutes in an informal competition with other shipbuilders!

Just before sleep one night that spring, I found myself comparing the historic mobilization of the nation in response to the very real threat of world domination by the forces of Nazism and the threats we faced in 2008, and still face today. Far-fetched? I didn't think so. The more I thought about it, the more I was certain that the two periods are closely aligned and that comparisons are relevant even to the present.

It is said that it took seven people working on the home front to support each man in battle overseas. That meant that we were *all* critical to the positive outcome of WWII. Every man, woman, and child had a role to play. And we did, even that little 20-year-old clerk named Betty in the Jim Crow union hall. Women moved into the workforce in large numbers for the first time, child labor laws were suspended so that children, too, could join in where feasible, families planted and maintained victory gardens to supplement limited civilian food supplies, elders acted as air-raid wardens and/or returned to the factories and canneries for the duration, my own grandfather Papa George among them.

WWII was our country's last *declared* war and the last time in our history when the *nation* went to war, not just the armed forces. Korea was called a "police action," and suitable euphemisms have covered every conflict since that time.

Today we live in a time, again, when the entire world is under threat. This time that threat is climate change. And this time it will take not only those of us living in the developed nations, but the entire world population to stave off the gradual extermination of human life from rising seas and changing physical environments. Maybe each *1 in the developed world* to *17 in emerging economies* odds will again be required in order to balance off all those good folks in faraway tropical climates waiting to own their first refrigerators and air conditioners! Whether we can *globally* respond in time remains a question. That we have already begun to see measurable signs of global warming is no longer in doubt.

The kind of general mobilization required to sustain life as we know it may lie in the history of the World War II home front as we lived it. The lessons were difficult to absorb since the speed with which we were forced to respond in order to survive the Nazi onslaught left little time or energy to incorporate them. It might be wise now to revisit that heroic period and take from it the models that served to reverse that crisis and make the world relatively safe again.

As Rosie once said, "We can do it!"

We know that because we did.

Blog Entry, January 10, 2009

Somewhere between the years of 11 and 13, there was a blinding insight that has been a major factor in the becoming of Betty for over a lifetime. This had to be associated with the absolutism of childhood combined with an awakening sense of social responsibility. The insight was life-altering and has been incorporated into a value system that persists to this day.

I recall that it was in that school assembly while reciting the Pledge of Allegiance that it hit me with the force of revealed "truth." I found myself instantly falling silent at the words "with Liberty And Justice For All." Not only that, but I continued to mouth the words while holding back the sounds. I recognized the phrase as absolutely untrue. I realized, perhaps for the first time, that the words didn't include me or anyone like me. I also realized, instinctively, that those young classmates standing around me with hand over heart and the piety of youth didn't know that. That the teacher whom I adored and who was leading the pledge was unaware, as well. I didn't know at that point where the blame should lie, but it wasn't with anyone there in that hall. That I was certain of, and I had no wish to dishonor their patriotism by allowing them to be witness to my dissent. I only knew that somewhere I'd read an anonymous quote: "Every day in every way, what I am to be I am now becoming." Words to live by. And with the passion of a small, well-read, and uncompromising little girl to support it, I would not participate in the lie. Not then, and not ever.

Later I would extend the practice to falling silent at the words *under God*, not because I'd intellectually worked my way out of religious orthodoxy—that would have required a far higher level of sophistication than I could claim—but because I found the words noninclusive of other belief systems (whose God?) and inserted into the pledge for all the wrong reasons. But that came much later, and from a far more reasoned place.

So that left two "audible" blanks in my personal pledge to my country, though I continued to rise in respect and participate to the extent that my values would allow. I'd never discussed this with anyone and presumed that I was alone in this practice of censoring and deleting as was appropriate to my personal beliefs.

On Inauguration Day in this year of 2009, I will stand and (for the first time since childhood) I will bring sound to the pledge. I'll take my place as one of "We the People," and I'll "promote the general welfare" and "form a more perfect Union," and boldly proclaim my part in the re-creation of all that may restore our once glorified and now badly tarnished image as the undisputed leader of the nations of the free world. And those words held suspect for so long will finally ring true.

And I'll do all that while witnessing the swearing in of the nation's first black president, completely awed by the arc of all our American lives that has brought us to this place of reconciliation and patriotism of a kind that now begins to make sense to those of us who have been silent and/or conditional in expressing it.

As I watch that historic national rite on Inauguration Day from the stands, I will be the only member of that audience of flag-pledging Americans who will know that I've uttered those words, *with liberty and justice for all!* aloud for the first time in over 70 years, and that I will be doing so as the full-fledged member of "We, the people!"

I REMEMBER LOOKING IN the bathroom mirror, as I prepared myself in the morning to attend Barack Obama's first inauguration, and seeing my mother there, which brought a grin as I recognized her. Where on earth had Betty gone to? Maybe it was a sign of fatigue that made me look and feel so much older on this day than I did the day before.

I slipped into my hip-length regulation raincoat with down inner lining zipped into place against the bitterness, topped it off with my very distinguished dimpled ranger Stetson, packed tissues into my pockets and dropped the little snapshot of Mammá, my enslaved great-grandmother, Leontine Breaux Allen, into my breast pocket. Mammá would share this day with me. It was for her as much as for myself that I was here at all. I was very much aware of her presence every minute of that historic day.

The front-page, lengthy *San Francisco Chronicle* article that had come out on the day before we left, with the headline "Biracial Ranger, 87, Heads to the Inauguration" and the line within that read "and she remembers her first bite of economic freedom in 1942 as one of the 'Rosie the Riveters' working in the World War II shipyards of Richmond" appeared to be the reporter's attempt at making me more relevant to the story of the day. I consider myself neither a Rosie nor biracial, except—as regards the biracial part—very peripherally. Somewhere, far back in the mid-1800s, that Mendelian link was probably forged and biracialism occurred in my Breaux-Charbonnet-Allen family tree. That would have been the result of the black-white African-Creole-Cajun-French-Spanish links.

I felt an undeniable kinship with President Obama when in his inaugural speech he mentioned that 60 years before, his own Kenyan father likely would have been refused service in the restaurants of Washington, and I recognized that, whatever else one might say about his biracial heritage, he was one of us, because he'd lived the black experience. It was then that the tears came and the kinship to power rained down. I searched for my cell phone and connected myself to my children back in Berkeley—in some magical way—to extend that power to them, too. And to my great-grandmother Leontine Breaux Allen, whose little picture was in my jacket pocket next to my heart. I knew my family was watching, and the unbelievable reach of technology in our times brought us all together, I sitting before the fantastic panorama unfolding before us at the nation's Capitol, and my family back home at the outer edge of the continent on the shores of the Pacific Ocean!

My identity as a black woman comes from the fact that—despite my ambiguous skin coloring that might make me appear to be almost anything—I have lived the black experience. That can never be erased, no matter how long I live. But I also suspect that my grandchildren may have lived into an era where that will no longer set them apart or bring them together any more than they will have need to claim it. The "black experience" has some years yet to go before we've grown past it as a nation, but in the meanwhile, it was impossible to walk among those millions of America's new best friends on the Mall and not feel that we've entered the age of poly-racialism and that we're going to have to find some new ways to discriminate if we're determined to keep alive the embers of the inequality that has cursed this nation for so long.

But for now, I remain a product of the "one-drop rule," which I cannot shed. I've lived too long and too painfully to allow myself to lose what is my greatest source of pride in these days of racial ambiguity. I've paid my dues to be able to survive on my own terms as a black woman. My children and grandchildren will confront their own times in their own ways. I pray that I've provided them a model of how that might be done, and that—however they identify—it will be with pride and dignity.

It's important to me, in the telling of my own story, to never forget that on both paternal and maternal lines is the awful reality of slavery. This is an authentic and shameful era of American history that is yet to be fully processed. Using that as a baseline, I could feel the enormous pride of having attained the right to witness the swearing in of the 44th president of these United States in the full realization that my chair was sitting but yards away from the dais, upon land that countless slaves had labored on without hope of freedom. They'd been hired out by their masters for the building of the magnificent Capitol building and the White House, the home that our new president and his young family were about to enter in this, his first term as the Leader of the Free World!

As crazy as it sounds, through tears of joy and disbelief, I felt a kinship with this remarkable young man and his family, knowing somewhere down deep that he will be stretched to the limits of his considerable capacities, but that his varied background, like my own, has prepared him well for all that lies ahead.

For right now, I'm still partially "up there," hovering in space, looking down upon a brand-new nation that was reborn on January 20 in that year of 2009. And I was feeling an essential part of humanity, this time without reservation, but only with unspeakable pride and joy and such a sense of humility and inadequacy in the face of what is yet to come.

Blog Entry, July 17, 2010

And then there was one.

My youngest sister, Lottie Charbonnet Balugo Fields, passed away this day—July 17, 2010, at around noon, on the 66th anniversary of the explosion at Port Chicago. We were attending the annual Day of Remembrance when word of her death came only moments after I arrived at home.

My eldest sister, Marjorie Charbonnet Brooms, left us many years ago in midlife. I'm not sure that I ever properly grieved over her loss, coming as it did during the time of the assassination of President Kennedy. Somewhere it all blended into some horrific nightmare. So many thoughts, both beautiful and troubling, as it is always with those of us left behind. How awful it is when time runs out on things unsaid . . .

I remember that when Uncle Louis, my father's younger brother, died, my dad was distressed that "God has sent his messengers to take away Louie out of sequence. I should have died first!"

Is that what I'm feeling: survivor's guilt?

I remember in 1987, while lying at the foot of my father's hospital bed as we shared his last hours, at the age of 92, having a blinding flash of insight that it might be just an illusion that medical science has extended human life. To me it seems more likely that what has been extended is death. His death process claimed the last 10 years of his previously productive life. My proud father spent his final decade blind and bedridden and totally dependent upon those around him.

I'm reminded that I was so grateful—even in grief—that Lottie didn't have a long period of lingering half alive and suffering in unmitigated agony. Though I have no idea how long she knew that the end was near or what fears she endured, the family had little warning before she slipped into eternity.

I remember the words of a dear poet friend, Benedict, on the death of my mother in 1995. The words were of little comfort then, but were so resoundingly true that I found a strange kind of peace in them despite their finality. He said, "Betty, we must remember that no life is complete without a death." At the time they didn't make sense to me, but in the days that followed—after the flowers were wilted and the mourning clothes put away—they were strangely comforting, and right.

I would never have been ready for this death since I could hardly imagine Lottie's life ending before mine. It just isn't fair, in the scheme of things. There was so much left unspoken, but maybe that's inevitably the way that fate has of keeping a "presence" alive, the essence of those who've passed on, a way to sustain life even in death. I suppose I'll be in silent and sometimes troubling conversation with my sister for as long as I'm alive.

I have another birthday in three weeks. After 70 they come every six weeks. Time is becoming more of a constant presence in my life. I'm considering giving it a name, and issuing it a serial number! How that which remains is spent is critically important, if only to me; not to be squandered.

I'M ONLY BEGINNING TO understand so much now that I have a life span to measure things against. That's one of the luxuries of being older. Really, it's incredible because you get to look back. It's like you get to live your life in blocks of time and then change comes. It's like reincarnation without ever leaving. So I get so now that I almost recognize the cycles changing, and I begin to feel the restlessness and begin to wonder what comes next. And it seems to come in 10- to 12-year cycles. And now I look back at those cycles and wonder how they were lived.

One day I had this sense of being simultaneously all the women that I ever was. And they all come out at different times depending on what's going on. But I'm aware of that now. I don't think it's something that I could have been aware of until I'd reached this age.

You only know it in retrospect, you don't see it coming up. But, now, it's the excitement of being an octogenarian and beyond. Because I have the luxury of coming from strong genes that go on for long periods, I have a sense of really having several more years of sentient living, and maybe I won't, but that's not the way my life is colored. I look at the next years and wonder, *What am I moving into now?* It keeps me propelling myself forward. Without being able to look at those long lives, on both sides, it's the slave women who had it. My father's great-grandmother, Marie Beaulieu, who was a mulatto and a slave, died at 101. My mother's grandmother, Leontine, died at 102. One of Mammá Leontine's daughters, Camille, went to 107, and my mother, Lottie, to 101. I don't have a sense, barring accidents, that this isn't another one of these periods. It's incredible!

My dad, God, I wish I could have a conversation with him at this stage of my life. There's so much I want to know that I'll never know now. I understand so much better his quiet times, his withdrawal, his formality, his huge pride. I understand it now.

My dad was a blind man. He lost his sight 10 years before he died. But I remember that my dad knew that the length from the top joint of his thumb to the tip was exactly one inch. And this precise quality about him—he could make home repairs and set things by using his finger. He would tell me, "You never go back and measure anything twice." He always told me that if you have to do that, you weren't careful in the first place. So my dad never retraced his steps. And I find that in myself; I never drive by the places I once lived in. I never retrace my steps. So I can see in myself the remnants of those stories from my father and my grandfather and I know what that's like.

That's what's so interesting to me, that one of the things that comes with getting older is losing the need to be that concrete, that you learn to live comfortably with conflicting truths, that when I was younger, something had to be this way or that way, but now they can be both.

BUT WHILE AGE DOES not wear on me, fame does.

I cannot begin to explain how unworthy it made me feel each time those piles of cards, letters, and thoughtful gifts loomed into view each morning as I sat sipping my tea with cereal and toast beside the harvest table that was now crowded with trophies and souvenirs, certificates of awards, proclamations, all undeserved, and reflecting my feelings of guilt at having accepted such honors from my community and the world! I *know* that folks need heroes, but why *me?* The crown does not sit comfortably on this graying head.

I decided that I must try to find the time soon or the weight of the guilt would follow me into my grave.

How one deals with this fame would probably cause havoc in the everyday existence of one far younger than I, yet here I was in my 90s trying to deal with it all at a time when I should have been concentrating on End of Life issues, right? The problem is that this is precisely where I found myself, thinking on all those levels and attempting to remain in the present. Impossible!

Over a span of several weeks in 2007, I remember being pursued by a high local public official who was anxious to have me co-host a television show that would focus on African American leaders who've contributed to local history over the decades. These would be the high achievers from the worlds of athletics, business, politics, education, etc., a kind of *Ebony* magazine of the airwaves, I guess, with its ever-constant listing of "First African Americans to . . ." whatever, or "Most eligible . . ." whatever, and ". . . breaks the color line!" All persons to be proud of, I'm sure. I guess I was waiting for the day when all of that will be ordinary and no longer news at all, because entry to the boardrooms, the athletic fields, and the halls of Congress will have been opened wide to all, when only *merit* will count.

I managed to find many ways to say no, without having much sense of why I felt so reluctant to join him. About the third time he approached me in my little cubbyhole of an office, I had decided to add to my refusal a recommendation as a way to pass the opportunity along to someone more in need of public exposure, someone who is young enough to still be building a résumé. It wasn't hard to come up with some possibilities who I was sure had the ability, the personal charm, the ambition, and the time to take this on and develop a new edge to their career goals.

He refused, and worked hard, mostly by appealing to my ego, to convince me that only *I* could provide what his vision of a fine program needed. And only *I* knew that was silly.

But I awoke one morning during that period realizing a wonderful thing: I was feeling completed these days, with a sense of no longer becoming. I'd entered a stage in life where I was now simply *being!* There was still a lot of work to do, don't misunderstand, and I was spending my days fully occupied in the process of "uploading" back into time everything that could be transferred back. However, I no longer needed any new starting places. I was busy tying up loose ends in the effort to *"leave the place better than I found it."* And there was nothing morbid about it. I was doing a hell of a job of giving back, and I'd found a venue in which to do that and am being given the platform and the tools that make it all possible.

I was aware in that dawn's early light that the lives of my enslaved great-grandmother, Leontine Breaux Allen, my mother, Lottie Allen Charbonnet, and I, Betty Charbonnet Reid Soskin, represented a span of time that embraces everything—all of the wars and social struggles and lynchings and fights for equality— from 1846 through today, just those three lives. Leontine lived from 1846 to 1948. Mother's life spanned the years from 1894 to 1995. I was born in 1921, and I'm still around. Leontine was born into a world population of less than 2 billion. Four generations later, I'm in a world population of nearly 8 billion. It's an awesome reality.

How I would *love* to have been able to see *their* stories—through the wonder of technology—in as much detail as I've been able to write of my own here.

Mammá could neither read nor write; her non-status as a slave prohibited it. She was freed at the age of 19, when the Emancipation Proclamation was signed. My own mother, Lottie, was barely able to read and very deliberately "drew" my school notes in scrawling, rounded letters using a tightly held pencil, having been taught primarily at night beside the oil stove by her not-much older Aunt Alice. Mother grew up as part of Mammá's household, where there were many children all needing to work the fields to raise the food for survival in that small shack beside the levee in St. James.

But even though I cannot see the details of their stories, it is their details that intertwined with mine and formed the fabric of my own life. So nothing of theirs has been lost.

And so here now, with a luxurious feeling of completion, as though I've enough superfluous life and talents left over from a life filled with trial and error, tragedy and pain, but with triumphs and personal achievements enough to balance it all out, enough to be able to leave behind a personal legacy that may enhance the lives of my children and theirs and, through my current work, the lives of others. And most of it is in intangibles, those things that are a part of the world by virtue of my having passed through, and I'm here by having entered through the wombs of those strong and good and forgiving and ever-reaching-upward heroic African American women.

I HAVEN'T A CLUE what my mother did for a living, but I think she did little. To the extent that she did work, she was a service worker. I know very little about my mother's educational background, if there was any at all. I'm not sure she went to school. Her education may have been purely by older members of the family. She had an aunt who lived in the same home she was raised in who created the first school for black children in St.

James Parish, Louisiana. So I think my mother's education was pretty much informal and guided by her Aunt Alice.

When she died in 1995 at the age of 101, I wrote in her obituary:

> You'll be remembered as a single bright feather on a pink silk hat aimed heavenward. Three-inch heels on moiré sandals with small red rose on toes. As a single, fragile butterfly in a windswept world of those too caught up to know your needs for touching and loving and caring, and most of all, for seeing your beauty. Bereft of worldviews, books unread, causes unserved, your time on earth was spent in simple ways, ways suited to a temperament shaped by your motherless beginnings that brought no models for your own mothering, but instilled a deep appreciation for family in its broadest sense, the legacy of that love-filled cabin in St. James, and your dear Mammá, who nurtured her brood with such warmth. It's that larger family that will miss your presence on this earth, family and friends of all ages, many of whom stayed with you through a long, long life as a replacement parent for those lost until the end game. I will miss you deeply, as we came full circle during your long lifetime, reversing roles, until near the end, you quite seriously introduced me to others as "Mother." Perhaps I became that in return at some point. You invariably made the correction, but I knew that no error had been made. We honor you in death as we loved you in life. Betty.

So when I get it all in perspective on a timeline, I can understand it and it makes sense to me.

That allows my mother's hunger to be seen, her crushing need, which is the thing that characterized her, the fact that she returned so easily to being a dependent after my father died. Because my father had been the caretaker for her for all the years of their marriage. She never left the child that had survived deep inside her. That child was always up front, demanding attention. I understood that.

From a relatively early age I seemed to have understood that she had never lived the hunger out. Her mother died when she was only seven months old. Throughout a troubled childhood, she was invisible in a household of many, many children. After the early death of her mother, Julia, her father moved on into a marriage and another family of four children—only to have his second wife, Desirée, pass on, too, returning those additional children to be also absorbed into Mammá's burgeoning household. I'm grateful that I began to get that sense of her before she died. That is why I wrote what I did in her obituary, which was that it was okay to let her be who she was.

And I really do remember her in that way with the feather, and that's okay, that was her role.

It was the early morning of July 1, 2016, my late mother's birthday, when I woke at one thirty to an intruder standing within six feet of my bed. I live in a second-floor apartment. He'd climbed up using the drainpipe, climbed over the railing, broken the lock on my sliding balcony doors, and entered surreptitiously in the night.

He was a slightly built white man, probably five foot seven to five foot nine, wearing a hoodie and, I suspect, lightweight pajamas. I knew that he was a white man because he spoke while trying to get me to stop screaming. I would have recognized a black male voice.

I rose from my bed with my cell phone in hand, but had no time to summon the police before it was wrested from my hand in a struggle that took us from the bedroom into the hallway with his arms pinning mine down and his hand over my mouth to silence my screams.

Had I been armed, my gun would have been taken from me in those same few seconds that my cell phone was knocked out of my hand and slung across the room. I might well have not survived.

He straddled my body as we struggled on the floor of the hallway and he beat me about the head and face with his fists, leaving bruises and a split lip that would last for days. As we struggled on the floor with me screaming as loudly as I could, to no response—I didn't know at the time that the two apartments downstairs were empty and there was no one to hear—but a sudden memory of defense strategies gave me the chance to reach into his loose-fitting pants and grab and squeeze his genitals as hard as I could. That caused him to back off, allowing me to escape to the nearby bathroom, where I immediately sat upon the floor with my feet propped against the door and my back against the cabinet housing the sink. I remembered that my electric iron was stored under the sink, let my feet loose for the few seconds it took to plug it into a wall outlet beside the sink, and turned the dial to linen—the hottest temperature—and sat while it quickly gained heat enough to brand the culprit for the police to find him once caught.

I have no idea where that power springs from under such circumstances, but I *do* know that as I sat down on that floor I was suddenly as calm as a cucumber, and I knew that I was going to survive this, that I was *surely* not a victim. Though I'd never had to know this before then, I had the distinct realization that I could take care of myself, and that this intruder was not going to be allowed to change my life, or to make me fear. I suspected that his beating me was for the purpose of silencing me, that he had no intention of killing me or seriously harming me, but I was interfering with his intent to steal items that he could sell and that, had I stopped screaming, or if I'd pretended sleep and allowed him to do his work, I might well have escaped personal harm.

I was told later that this is a "victim's" way of blaming oneself and not a healthy attitude, but I suspect that I'm right.

As I sat for about 30 minutes in that bathroom, listening for signs of activity, he was busy going through my apartment, picking up items—my computer, my iPhone, a lovely hand-painted bamboo fan and teak box beautifully adorned with abalone shells received as gifts from the South Korean National Park Service for an article I'd written for their journal, the presidential coin presented to me by President Barack Obama at the national tree-lighting ceremony the previous December, challenge coins collected over time and gathered together in a small wine-colored velvet drawstring bag that laid on the table in my living room, along with other personal treasures.

Of the items, it was that presidential coin that I treasured most and felt most the loss of.

The physical bruises were not serious enough to require a physician's attention, though the fire and police departments were well represented in my living room within a few minutes. After I was sure that the intruder had left, I pounded on the apartment door across from mine, and, despite the late hour (around 1:00 A.M.), they answered the door and summoned the police for me.

They were outraged! My community was outraged! I think that I just felt lucky to have survived the encounter.

I was distraught, but held together until late the next morning when—after a sleepless night—I fell totally apart . . .

EVER SINCE THE HOME intrusion, there has been this corner of my dining alcove where an accumulation of large plastic bags are stowed that hold the countless cards of best wishes, gifts from well-wishers from every corner of the nation, all waiting appropriate thank-you notes of acknowledgement.

For a few evenings after the incident, dear friends came with their own well-wishes, offering to help me read through them. We did that for several healing evenings, with every intention of continuing until we'd properly expressed gratitude, but that came to a natural end after I returned to work and to a calendar now crowded with future commitments that I've been dutifully fulfilling ever since. The publicity created new exposure in parts of the world previously beyond my experience, and this was followed by trips of an amazing several days spent in Telluride, Colorado, participating in the Mountainfilm festival, then a few days later on to the National World War II Museum in New Orleans to be honored along with others from that era, followed by 10 days in Washington, D.C., for the opening of the new National Museum of African American History and Culture. All of that was packed into just a few weeks, and in between, my three-times-a-week presentations in our little theater in the park's Visitor Education Center have gathered a following that is running at capacity. *Hamilton* has nothing on us except a much larger theater. Ours only holds 48 seats, but we're sold out at each performance!

But Life has never felt richer, despite all.

I WOKE ONE MORNING in the spring of 2017 to clarity and self-confidence. I'd been aware for almost a year that I would be awarded an Honorary Doctorate at the spring commencement of the California College of the Arts in San Francisco. When the announcement originally came it was a complete surprise, and I truly felt that some error had been made at a very high level. I'd never attended college at all, and I didn't even know anyone at CCA, at least no one that I was aware of at the time. I'd been told that there would be 4,000 attending. It was unimaginable! Surely someone would discover this monstrous mistake before the month of May!

Included in the announcement packet was a list of former recipients, which only added to my confusion. The list was long and included many iconic figures of the worlds of arts and literature.

I'd go to sleep each night thinking about what I would say in my commencement address and completely intimidated by the prospect of what lay ahead.

Not sure what brought this euphoric state about on this particular morning, or even if I could rely upon its staying power, but the words lined up as if by magic. I knew their meaning, and that there was little need to try to organize them further. Over the days that were to come—between then and the day of the commencement—they would continue to sort themselves out and deepen. They were relevant to this graduating class, I believed. The title, "Thumbprints, Gateposts, and Bookends," was the key that opened the door into the connections not only to my past, but to the arts. As suspected, they were there all the time, sitting behind my eyes, waiting for me to settle down and listen to myself, maybe . . .

Those "gateposts" are key to one of the family stories about my great-grandmother Mammá, a precious memory from childhood, one of the many stories told by Papa George as we tied the string beans to their poles and dug up the carrots and gathered the melons in that little kitchen garden after my parents and we three children arrived in Oakland, escaping from the New Orleans floods of 1927.

My impression of what romance meant was formed very early in childhood. It was the Civil War story of Leontine sitting high in the branches of a pecan tree that stood beside the family's long front porch, my great-grandmother watching the Union soldiers marching past on that dusty road from Donaldsonville. She must have been very young, perhaps 16 or 17, and from her photographs, quite pretty. I knew that she was barely five feet tall, so the exciting tale of the soldier, Corporal George Allen of one of the Louisiana regiments of the United States Colored Troops, stepping out of the line long enough to coax her down from her perch, then rejoining the march carrying her on his shoulders for a few miles, was not hard to believe. He would later become her husband and father of their dozen or so children. This would be the standard for love stories that Hollywood would have to meet in order to gain my little-girl approval. And it was *true*.

That the child Betty heard such lovely stories far earlier in life than stories of the unspeakable brutality of slavery or the great Civil War that brought it to an end means that I had little awareness of my great-grandmother as being enslaved. Nor do I recall making that *personal* connection until studying American history as an adolescent. But the intellectual connections rarely mean as much as the emotional imprinting, and there is little memory of making those linkages. If the elders of the family spoke of such times, they must have done so in Creole, a patois of French that dominated speech in our homes during those years and placed such conversations out of reach of the children. Perhaps it was just too painful. They could hardly have not been scarred by such memories, but I can't recall feeling a personal relationship to that tragic history of slavery until I was a young mother, when I, too, held it at arm's length from my own children, until the '60s.

I only remember Mammá as the family matriarch, celebrated by the elders as the aunts and uncles made up the delegation that would make the trip back to St. James Parish each year for her birthday. Southern Pacific Railroad family passes enabled this important family ritual to continue for decades, since most uncles were redcaps or porters during the Great Depression. Wonderful stories about their childhood in that little cabin across from the levee of the Mississippi, where my grandfather and my mother and her siblings and so many others were raised, fueled most grown-up conversations and colored my childhood memories, and surely provided the foundation for how I relate to "the World."

I no longer worried about what I would say at the commencement exercises. These were the stories and life lessons I would share.

EPILOGUE

Betty's Cbreaux Speaks *blog had a core of hundreds of loyal followers that was growing steadily, and she was becoming an increasingly sought-after speaker at various schools and organizations around the Bay Area on such topics as aging, black history, and Bay Area World War II home front history. But her national—and even international—celebrity status did not take off until the fall of 2013, when her supervisor at the Rosie the Riveter park asked her to do an Associated Press interview on the Republican-sponsored shutdown of the federal government. "The rest is history," Betty wrote in her blog. "Within hours of the AP story's publication the excitement began!"*

She immediately became the face of both the National Park Service and of an entire nation shut out from their federal government, with a sudden scramble of reporters and interviewers and media personnel all wanting to get her in their news outlets or on their programs.

She wrote: "Our visitation has soared, and more and more people are coming in as the result of having heard of Rosie the Riveter/WWII National Historical Park for the first time only recently, and one gets the feeling that I've become the poster girl for senior centers from coast to coast! Beside that, the only thing that seems to have happened is that almost everyone who turns up at our visitor center mentions having seen me on local or national news programs, and never have I had so many requests of folks wanting to have me take snapshots with them for sending home to family and friends.

"One might think that the end of the national Shutdown might have brought an end to the splash of publicity but, to the contrary, it seems only the beginning."

Indeed. As many in the nation discovered this remarkable woman, still working full-time in her 90s, imparting the collected wisdom of almost a century of life, so authentic in a time of so many fake celebrities, what followed was her blog readership soaring into the thousands along with a string of recognitions, awards, and honors, culminating in her being chosen as the person to introduce President Barack Obama at the National Tree Lighting Ceremony in Washington, D.C., in December 2015 and receiving an honorary doctorate at Oakland's California College of the Arts a year later. This for a woman who had never gone to college but was busy about her business of educating the nation.

And she responded in typical, self-effacing Betty style.

"Having become a nationally recognizable public figure has meant accepting responsibility for never leaving the house without checking first to see that my socks match (easy when they're all government regulation and identical) and that I've remembered to attach all my ID tags so that they're both visible and lined up properly on my jacket."

AFTER SOME MONTHS OF sitting with my own thoughts, alone, my blog began to slowly become the mechanism by which I could hold conversations with myself as I processed life. There was never an outside presence standing in judgment. I cannot recall any time when it ever came up in conversation with any family members. I thought that it would surely hold little interest among the young until after my death.

Oddly enough, neither did I ever become aware of or write to a *public* audience. I never invited criticism, permission, arguments for or against anything. It just became a method of ordering my life as it was being lived—processing fears and resentments, concerns, both public and private. I opined about everything large and small, so that I might leave at least an impression of my having shared life on the planet, and that I contributed in tiny increments either by what I did or failed to do toward creating the future, along with everybody else on the planet. No more, no less.

Even though I later became aware that this personal journal developed a worldwide following over time, I still tended to write without being consciously aware of whoever was out there reading my words. I was usually sitting at my computer, alone at the end of my day, generally in my pajamas and slipper socks with a single library lamp at my elbow dimly lit, and in conversation with myself while letting others listen.

There has never been any particular order to any of it, no rhyme or reason, just a way of explaining Life to myself while in the process of living it. I rarely went back to reread anything I'd written, finding that I'd expended all of the energy of it in the original documenting of the thoughts. Once written, however, I found those thoughts committed to memory for all time, as with all of the songs I've ever composed, despite the fact that they were rarely written down or published anywhere. Because there are few stated rights or wrongs, there was little reason for making corrections. The magic, the power, appears to be embedded in the act of creation for me, whatever the form.

In a strange way, my journal appeared to be propelling me forward into an unknown future with intentionality. It brought a sense of order to my life—though never with a conscious awareness of the unfolding process—only in the sense that for me, for this hour, in this moment, and though it is always subject to revision in the light of new realities, this is my *Truth*.

But I've been giving some thought to this writing business, as a potentially *serious* author, that is. The keeping of a journal has its appeal, I suppose, but one has to assume that an otherwise disinterested public wants to hear what one has to say. That's a big question. It takes a lot of ego to subscribe to that, maybe more than I have.

I understand and appreciate the appeal of Toni Morrison, Alice Walker, Terry McMillan, and Zora Neale Hurston. Their writings describe black life, in many cases in the vernacular of the black experience. I suppose that my admiration for their abilities has prevented me from even *considering* myself capable of consideration as being worthy of the title *author*. My voice may be so *atypical*, with such an atypical story to tell, that there will be no audience wanting to know. A hybrid of the times. After all, I'm still working my way out of feeling as though, racially, I'm *nothing*. But I've finally decided that, in fact, I'm really *everything*, and it's a wonderful thing to be, after all. At least that's the way I see my beautifully blended grandchildren.

My life experiences are in many ways a mirror of those of countless other African Americans who are members of the middle class, brought up to middle-class mores and values. We're often the beneficiaries of a wide variety of cultures by virtue of miscegenation and greater access to sociopolitical life, and are often placed in positions that allow us to effect social change disproportionately, if we opt to use them in that way. We find ourselves being sought after to validate racial diversity on boards and commissions everywhere, often for the simple reason that we're seen as "not like those others." Many of us fall prey to ego by believing that we represent more than that. One of the most painful lessons I learned in life as a black woman in white suburbia was that the concept of a middle-class black exists only in the mind of a middle-class black. To most of the rest of the country, a nigger is a nigger is a nigger! An architect-designed home, a backyard swimming pool, a wood-paneled station wagon, Armani suits, and vacations in Hawaii or Palm Beach do not a member of the elite make, despite arguments to the contrary. Acceptance is invariably conditional.

Perhaps my value and marketability as a writer will lie in the fact that mine may be a relatively unheard voice. Maybe it's one of the voices of the future, a forerunner of a nation forced to write new rules of conduct to cover a country going "beige," with new guidelines created to maintain white superiority in a nation where skin color or lack thereof is fast losing power to control governance. It's a revolutionary thought, and one that is already bending the rules of the game. There is hope in the knowledge that many ordinary Americans are now beginning to see the fallacy in white supremacy and that its protection cannot be maintained without sacrificing democracy itself.

There are millions of us out there growing up in a world forever affected by the revolutionary social changes of the past 50 years. We've *already* changed the world for the better, though if you don't know where to look, you won't know that.

One of the exciting signs for me is that when I'm sitting with other elders who are veterans of the political and social battles of bygone days, I see good folks still working hard to bring about racial equality for all the right reasons. But it's still a *goal* to be attained at great risk and personal sacrifice. If I cross town into Oakland to sit in on a poetry jam at the Black Dot Café or the Malonga Casquelourd Center, or the Yerba Buena Center for the Arts in San Francisco, or the East Bay Center for the Performing Arts in Richmond, young people of every color, racial, or ethnic group, gender orientation, economic class, and educational background can be seen with their eyebrow rings, skullcaps, and baggy pants, sharing their poetry in a world where those differences have been relegated to a back seat and equality is simply *assumed*. They're not really *working* at it anymore. It's called the hip-hop world, and that world has *already* arrived. It's standing on spindly, wobbly legs like a newborn colt, but it's here. The Internet is giving it strength. The arts are giving it form. And in many ways, I can recognize it because at the Nu Upper Room in Oakland, I along with others acted as a midwife to its birth. We weren't alone. In many corners of the country it's been coming alive simultaneously, struggling to be heard above the din of a war that wants to crush them out to still their voices.

It's a matter of stepping ahead with them into a future that they're busily creating. The young *know*. And, just as that remarkable group of socially venturesome intellectuals and spiritual gurus in the late '70s and early '80s arrived in the greater Bay Area in large enough numbers to establish the Human Potential Movement in the wake of the Free Speech Movement and the Freedom Summer of the explosive '60s, there is now a critical mass of youth doing the same for racial equality and environmental and criminal justice in the new millennium. It's the magic of the self-fulfilling prophecy. Through its magic, the Bay Area has been transformed for the better and been radiating out into the country and the world ever since.

Maybe I'll be worth reading because mine is a voice of hope. I've seen the future in the faces of the young and my only wish is that I could hang around and live it with you.

Maybe—as a translator of the language of social change over a great expanse of time—my voice is one of the carriers of history and a reliable predictor of the future.

Maybe because, for whatever reason, I've remained politically and experientially black despite the seduction of expediency and the quest for personal fortune.

Maybe because I've retained the ability to *say* and *be* what I *am* and what *it is* with candor and without restraint—mine is another black voice to be read and heard alongside the rest.

Maybe because a deviant voice adds breadth and depth to and expands the black experience.

Maybe this is the time to speak beyond the listeners at my shoulder and in the boardrooms before it's too late and time runs out, and just maybe this is a gentle way of avenging the cruel enslavement of my ancestors Celestine "of no last name" and Leontine Breaux Allen, into whose shoes I've stepped in *my* time by giving them legitimate voices beyond the grave and into the continuum of family and national history.

. . . And there it is!

My reason to write, that which only *I* will have lived and documented because only *I* have lived *their* lineage down through all of the drama of all of the generations and into *my* humble shoes!

But where do I go from here . . . ?

INDEX

A

Abbott, Robert S., 141
academia, 118–119
Air Force, 41–42
Albers Mill, 24
Allen, Albert, 163
Allen, Desirée Fernandez, 13, 178
Allen, George ("Papa George"; grandfather), 12–13, 18, 19, 21, 23, 29–31, 34, 152, 162–165, 182
Allen, George, Jr., 13
Allen, Julia "Minette," 13, 178
Allen, Leontine Breaux ("Mammá"; great-grandmother), 4, 10–15, 168, 169, 173, 175, 176, 182–183, 190
Allen-Jernigan, Vivian, 14, 18, 19, 29, 30
American Friends Service Committee, 100
Anderson, Maxwell, 32, 79
Aroner, Dion, 121, 131, 136, 149
Arroyo Del Valle preventorium, 28

B

Baldwin, James, 29
Baraka, Amiri, 123

Barton, Cheryl, 136
Bay Area, 17–34, 46–47, 50, 110n, 122, 138, 152, 154, 189
Beaulieu, Marie, 173
Before the Mayflower (Bennett), 95
Bennett, Lerone, 95
Bidleman, Carl, xiii
Big Olga, 4–5
Bilal, Mohammed, 124
Bilal, Rafiq, 121–124
Birmingham church bombing, 92
black colleges, 141
black experience, 169, 187, 190
black history, 141–142, 153
"Black Log" (Soskin), 164
Black Panther Party, 96–97
Black Power Movement, 95
Black Unitarian Universalist Caucus, 94, 95
Boilermakers Union, 43–45, 132–134, 136n, 138, 153, 158, 165
Bortin, David, 62–65
Breaux, Celestine, 10–11, 14, 190
Breaux, Edouard, 10–11, 14
Breaux, Sylvestre, 11
Breaux, Theophile, 11
Byron Rumford Plaza, 120–122

C

Caesar, Shirley, 50

Cajuns, 9–11, 145

California College of the Arts (CCA), 181–183, 186

California Golden Eagles, 35

California State Assembly, 15, 121, 131, 136, 138, 149

Carver, George Washington, 141

Castlemont High School, 31–34, 37, 65, 139

Castro, Eddie, 32

Catholicism, 4, 17–18, 26–27, 65, 82–85, 87, 108, 111

CBreaux Speaks blog, xi, xii, 112, 143–148, 153–155, 166–168, 171–172, 185–187

Chaney, James, 163n

Charbonnet, Armand, 7

Charbonnet, Dorson Louis (father), 1, 2, 4–6, 9, 13, 18, 22–26, 28, 34, 55, 61–62, 108, 145, 146, 173

   illness and death of, 88, 89, 105, 127, 128, 171, 173, 177

Charbonnet, Lottie (sister), 1, 2–3, 27, 50, 51

   death of, 171–172

Charbonnet, Lottie Allen (mother), 4–5, 9, 10, 13, 14, 18, 20, 26, 30–32, 34, 37, 38, 86–88, 168, 173, 175–178

   Betty's obituary for, 177, 178

   illness and death of, 88, 89, 127, 130, 172, 177, 178

Charbonnet, Louis (grandfather), 1, 2, 6, 7, 145–146

Charbonnet, Louis (uncle), 6, 171

Charbonnet, Louis, III, 147

Charbonnet, Marjorie ("Margie"; sister), 1, 7, 18, 27, 32, 50, 51

   death of, 93–94, 171

Charbonnet, Melbourne, 8

Charbonnet, Patricia, 8

Charbonnet, Paul, 6

Charbonnet, Victoria Morales ("Mamair"; grandmother), 2–5, 21

Chicago Defender, 141

Child from One to Five, The (Gesell and Ilg), 68

Civil Rights Act, 66

Civil Rights Movement, 91–98, 108, 157, 163

Civil Service Commission, 40–41, 44

Civil War, 35, 158–159, 182

Clark Sisters, 50

Cleaver, Eldridge, 96

Cleaver, Kathleen, 96

Cleveland, James, 50

climate change, 165–166

Coker, Raleigh, 3

Coleman, Steve, 123

communism, 40–41, 65

Concord Weapons Station, 100

Condon, Eleanor, 57–58

Condon, Robert, 57–58

Corpus Christi Catholic Church, 4–5, 6, 145

Creoles, 2, 4–9, 20, 21, 24–27, 31, 32, 75, 145, 182

Cullen, Mrs. Countee, 95

D

Dean, Shirley, 119–20

Democratic National Convention, 92, 107

Depression, 20, 23, 78, 183

Depression Beach, 23

Detroit, Mich., 1, 7, 22, 110n

Dewson, Dick, 25

Diablo Valley, 67, 94, 96–97

Diller, Howard, 92

Duhl, Leonard, 8

E

East Oakland, Calif., 18–19, 25–26, 30, 31, 37, 59, 67
  Nu Upper Room in, 121–125, 189
Ebony, 95
"Ebony the Night" (Soskin), 95–96
Edwin Hawkins Singers, 107–108
Ellington, Duke, 4, 25, 49
Eugene O'Neill National Historic Site, 157

F

Farallon Islands, 80
Father Divine, 56–57
FBI, 41
Fielding, Ruth, 28
Five Blind Boys of Mississippi, 50
Franklin, Aretha, 50
Franklin, C. L., 50
Freedom Summer, 91, 98, 189
Fujioka, George, 92

G

Gaillard, Slim, 49
Galt, William Henry, 35
gay marriage, 128–130
Gesell, Arnold, 68
Gibel, Bryan, xv
GI bill, 56
Gilbert, Al, 66–67
Gilbert, Bessie, 60–61, 66–67
Gilbert, Evelyn, 67
Gilbert, Jimmy, 67
Gilmartin, Aron, 94–97, 99–101
global warming, 165–66
Golden Gate National Cemetery, 155–156
Good Friday, 18

Goodman, Andrew, 163n
Great Depression, 20, 23, 78, 183
Gregory Gardens Improvement Association, 62–65, 105, 106
Grosjean's Mill, 24

H

Haiti, 6
Hamer, Fanny Lou, 92
Hampton, Henry, 95
Hancock, Loni, 121, 138, 149
Harris, Wynonie, 48
Hart, Judy, 132
Hawaiian Warriors, 35, 86
Hawkins, Erskine, 49
Higgins, Gordon, 128–129
hip-hop, 123, 189
Holiday, Billie, 49
Holy Family Sisters, 6, 146
Hope, John, 141
Hopkins, Lightnin', 31, 49
Hurricane Katrina, 144–148
Hurston, Zora Neale, 187
Hydel, Dr., 14

I

Ilg, Frances L., 68
Isleños, 2, 5

J

Jackson, Jesse, 95
Jelinek, Don, 120
John Muir National Historic Site, 157
Johnson, James Weldon, 29
Johnson, Lyndon, 92, 110
Johnson, Robert Henry, 123
Jordan, Louis, 4, 49

K

Kahn, Albert, 150
Kaiser, Henry J., 46, 140–141, 164–165
Kelly, Terrance, 142
Kennedy, John F., 93–94, 97, 110, 171
Khayyám, Omar, xi
Killen, Edgar Ray, 162–163
King, Martin Luther, Jr., 97
King, Robin, 101–104
Konte, Keba, 123
Korean War, 49, 165
KRE (radio station), 48
Ku Klux Klan, 132–133, 163

L

Last Poets, 123
Liberty ships, 141
Long, Huey, 8
Louisiana, 2, 5, 8–10, 13, 14, 18n, 26, 27, 110n. *See also* New Orleans, La.
 St. James Parish, 9–11, 13–15, 163, 176–177, 183
L'Ouverture, Toussaint, 6, 141
Lunceford, Jimmie, 4, 25, 49
lynching, 89, 147, 163

M

Madame Butterfly, 8
Malcolm X, 97
Mandela, Nelson, 148
Mardi Gras, 27, 147
Martin Luther King Jr. Regional Shoreline Park, 19
Marxism, 99
McCracklin, Jimmy, 31
McGovern, George, 107
McMillan, Terry, 187
"Meditation" (Soskin), 76, 77

Millay, Edna St. Vincent, 28, 78
Miller, Dorie, 141
Mingus Amungus, 123
minstrel shows, 59–61
Mississippi Freedom Democratic Party (MFDP), 92
Mitford, Jessica, 57n
Moore's Dry Dock, 140n
Morrison, Toni, 187
Moyers, Bill and Judith, 125
Mt. Diablo Unitarian Universalist Church, 62, 65, 98
Mueller, Mr. and Mrs., 19
Musso, Aldo, 48

N

NAACP, xiii
National Conference of Black Unitarian Universalists, 94, 95
National Museum of African American History and Culture, 180
National Park Service, 131, 133, 148, 157
 Betty's work with, xiv, xvi, 15, 121, 131–143, 148–157, 180–181, 185
 civic engagement and, 151
 Rosie the Riveter/World War II Homefront National Historical Park, xiv, xvi, 15, 121, 131–143, 149, 154, 155, 157, 159, 185
 structures and, 135–137
National Women's History Project, 15
National World War II Museum, 180
New Orleans, La., 1–15, 20, 22, 23, 33
 Hurricane Katrina in, 144–148
 storm and flood in, 17–18, 23
Newport, Gus, 119–120
Newton, Huey, 96
Nu Upper Room, 121–125, 189

O

Oakland Army Induction Center, 101–103

Oakland Athletic Club, 18, 21, 29

Oakland Giants, 35, 86

Obama, Barack, 168–170, 179, 186

Of Lost Conversations and Untold Stories, 159, 160

Olga (cousin), 4–5

Operation PUSH, 95

P

Parker, Edward, 35

Parkmead Elementary School, 59

Parks, Rosa, xi

Patterson, William, 35–36

Patton, George, 141

PBS, 91, 92, 95

Pearl Harbor, 141

Peterson, Charles, 80–82

Pinel School, 69–70, 73

Pleasant Hill, Calif., 62

Pledge of Allegiance, 166–167

Port Chicago, Calif., 157
    explosion at, 45–46, 155–157, 171
    war protest at, 100–101

Powelson, Marian, 59–60

Power, Will, 123, 125

Project Community, 110, 118

Q

Quakers, 100

R

Rawls, Lou, 49

redlining, 116

Red Oak Victory, SS, 150, 164–165

Reid, Bob (son), 51, 53, 55, 59, 61, 65, 66, 69, 72, 73, 77, 85, 101–103, 105, 107
    Rick and, 130

Reid, Dale Richard ("Rick"; son), 51–53, 55, 58–59, 61, 65, 66, 68, 70–72, 93, 107, 114, 126–130
    as adopted child, 48, 50–51, 68, 70–72, 83–84
    death of, 127, 129–130
    Higgins and, 128–129
    Mel and, 51, 52, 71–72, 108, 109, 113
    Ron and, 126–127
    sexual identity of, 51–53, 70–72, 77, 88, 89, 107

Reid, David (son), 24, 51, 53, 55, 59, 61, 65, 66, 69, 72, 73, 77, 85, 107
    Rick and, 127–130

Reid, Dorian (daughter), 92
    birth of, 53–54, 61
    disability of, 53, 54, 68–70, 77, 78, 88, 89, 107
    schooling of, 69–70, 107

Reid, Mel (first husband), 34–36, 39–41, 43, 45, 46, 48, 50, 55, 59, 62, 67, 82, 86–90, 94, 98, 106–109, 111
    athletic career of, 35, 42, 50, 86, 87, 128
    Betty's marriage to, 27, 38–39, 55, 77, 79, 83, 86–88, 106, 108, 161
    Betty's meeting of, 34
    Betty's separation and divorce from, 79, 87–90, 106–109, 111, 161
    death of, 90, 105, 128, 162
    diabetes of, 109, 113–115, 128
    family of, 35–36
    gambling of, 107, 109
    Navy enlistment of, 39, 42–43
    record store of, 48–51, 61, 75, 86, 107, 109–110, 113–115

Rick and, 51, 52, 71–72, 108, 109, 113

Reid, Paul, 49–50, 109

Reid, Tom, 34

Reid's Records, 48–51, 61, 75, 86, 107, 109–10, 113–117, 119, 120

Richert (sailor), 45–46

Richmond, Calif., 131–134, 142, 150–151, 160, 163

    Boilermakers Union in, 43–45, 132–134, 136n, 138, 153, 158, 165

    Iron Triangle district of, 149–150

    Kelly murder in, 142

    Ku Klux Klan in, 132–133

    population of, 46, 132, 137, 140, 150–151

    Rosie the Riveter/World War II Homefront National Historical Park in, xiv, xvi, 15, 121, 131–43, 149, 154, 155, 157, 159, 185

    shipyards at, 44, 46, 131–141, 150–151, 164–165, 168

Robert E. Peary, SS, 165

Robeson, Paul, 35–36

Robinson, Jackie, 32

Rose, Charlie, 125

Rosie the Riveter, 134, 136, 137, 141, 153, 157–158, 160, 166, 168

Rosie the Riveter/World War II Homefront National Historical Park, xiv, xvi, 15, 121, 131–143, 149, 154, 155, 157, 159, 185

Ross, Jennifer, 123

Rumford, Byron, 121

S

Sacramento Street, 39, 46, 113, 115, 117, 119–121

Sacramento Zouaves, 35

St. James Parish, 9–11, 13–15, 163, 176–177, 183

St. Louis Cathedral, 146–147

St. Mary's Catholic Church, 65

Sanford, Don, 97–98

Sanford, Susan, 97–99

San Francisco Bay, 80

San Francisco Bay Area, 17–34, 46–47, 50, 110n, 122, 138, 152, 154, 189

San Francisco Chronicle, 168

San Francisco–Oakland Bay Bridge, 79, 81

San Pablo Park, 34, 35, 152–153

Schwartzenberg, Susan, 136

Schwerner, Michael, 163n

segregation, 5

Shakiri, Sister, 123

sharecroppers, 89

"Sign My Name to Freedom" (Soskin), 97–99

Sisters of the Holy Family, 6, 146

16th Street Baptist Church, 92

slavery, 10–14, 170, 176, 182–183

Smith, Rick, 138–139

Smith, Sewall, 56

Soskin, Betty Charbonnet Reid

    Air Force job of, 41–42

    awards and honors of, 181–183, 186

    birth of, 1, 175

    blog of, xi, xii, 112, 143–148, 153–155, 166–168, 171–172, 185–187

    Boilermakers Union job of, 43–45, 132–134, 136n, 138, 153, 158, 165

    childhood of, 1–4, 17–31

    Civil Service Commission job of, 40–41, 44

    domestic servant job of, 37–38

    as emancipated woman, 105–106, 128, 162

    fame of, ix–x, 174–175, 180, 185–186

family history of, 5–6, 9–15, 22, 143–147, 169

films about, xiii–xv

in high school, 31–34, 37, 65, 139

home intruder and, 178–180

home lost by, 109, 110

honorary doctorate of, 181–183, 186

identity as black woman, 169–170

interview on government shutdown, 185

luncheon speeches given by, 82

marriages of. *See* Reid, Mel; Soskin, William F. "Bill"

mental breakdown of, 75–79, 106

name of, 161–162

National Park Service work of, xvi, xviii, 15, 121, 131–143, 148–157, 180–181, 185

panic attacks and blackouts experienced by, 79–81

political life and activism of, 15, 91–104, 107, 115–117, 119–121, 136, 138, 149

reading of, 28–29

record store of, 48–51, 61, 75, 86, 107, 109–110, 113–117, 119, 120

Rosie the Riveter/World War II Homefront National Historical Park and, xiv, xvi, 15, 121, 131–143, 149, 154, 155, 157, 159, 185

singing and songwriting of, 28–29, 75–76, 78–82, 85–86, 97–99, 108, 111–112, 121, 162, 164, 187

at tuberculosis preventorium, 28

in Walnut Creek, 55–64, 75, 76, 82, 88, 89, 96, 101, 109–111, 119

Soskin, William F. "Bill," 8, 114, 118, 146, 161

Betty's divorce from, 126

Betty's marriage to, 88, 90, 111, 115, 118–119, 161–162

Betty's meeting of, 110

Betty's songwriting and, 111–112

Buddhist monastery entered by, 126

death of, 126, 128, 162

Project Community of, 110, 118

Southern Pacific Railroad, 18, 20, 22, 183

Staple Singers, 50

Stokes, Carl, 95

Student Nonviolent Coordinating Committee, 98, 163n

T

Telluride Mountainfilm, 180

Third Baptist Church, 35

Thoreau, Henry David, 103

Three Blind Mice, 25

Torres, Naomi, 143

Treuhaft, Robert, 57

Triangle Shirtwaist Factory, 159

Truman, Harry, 157

tuberculosis, 28

Tubman, Harriet, 141

Tuskegee Airmen, 141

U

Unitarian church, 82, 84–85, 94–96, 108, 110

Mt. Diablo Unitarian Universalist Church, 62, 65, 98

Unitarian-Universalist Association, 94–95

United Nations, 35

United Service Organizations (USOs), 45

University of California at Berkeley, xii, xiv, 18, 32, 75, 110, 111, 162

Project Community at, 110, 118

Untold Stories, 159, 160

V

Vaughn, Sarah, 49
Victory ships, 141
Vietnam War, 100–103
Voting Rights Act, 92

W

Walker, Alice, 187
Walnut Creek, Calif., 55–64, 75, 76, 82, 88, 89, 96, 101, 109–111, 119
Walnut Festival, 92–93
Warnie, Isabel Allen LeBeouf, 10
Warnie, Joe ("Daddy Joe"), 29
War on Poverty, 92
Washington, Dinah, 49
Washington, Kenny, 32
We Charge Genocide (Patterson), 35
Williams, Cecil, 122
Wilson, Brian, 101
Wilson, Dorothy, 56

Wilson, Lionel, 56
Winterset (Anderson), 32, 79
Wonder Bread, 34
working women, 158–159, 165
World War I, 158–159
World War II, 39, 40, 43, 47, 92, 131–132, 134, 135, 153–154, 165, 166
 African Americans in, 141, 147
 Betty's work at Boilermakers Union during, 43–45, 132–134, 136n, 138, 153, 158, 165
 Rosie the Riveter, 134, 136, 137, 141, 153, 157–158, 160
 Rosie the Riveter/World War II Homefront National Historical Park, xiv, xvi, 15, 121, 131–143, 149, 154, 155, 157, 159, 185
 shipyards and war plants during, 39, 40–41, 43, 44, 46, 131–141, 150–151, 164–165, 168
 and women in workforce, 158, 165

ACKNOWLEDGMENTS

IN LOOKING BACK ON a long life lived precariously at times, there were and continue to be those who held the lantern to light the way when needed. The first was surely my great-grandmother, Leontine Breaux Allen, the much-loved Mammá of my childhood. I am one of many descendants whose lives were influenced by that dear soul who survived slavery and left her mark on us all.

Reverend Aron Gilmartin, a Unitarian Universalist minister, provided the guidance that brought me through the civil rights revolution of the Sixties. That turbulent period might well have left me shattered along the roadside. However, in large part because of Rev. Gilmartin's help, I emerged from that period virtually unscathed, though forever changed by the momentous events of those years that brought my small life into harmony with the national narrative and daring to break through the stereotypes into myself.

In these final decades there have been National Park Service colleagues Jonathan Jarvis, Martha Lee, and Tom Leatherman, who, together and sequentially, guided me through these last years where I have found meaning in a continuing life and where I've been fully and unconditionally supported, and who provided me with a platform from which to proclaim my Truths to a nation now ready to receive them.

And to my sons, Bob and David, and daughter, Dorian, whose love has given me the power and strength to live into these final years with a sense of purpose and dedication to principles that took 96 years to fully form into a personal faith that has endured.

Together, they all have allowed me the sense and privilege of having lived into a future that I've helped to create.

Finally, I want to give special thanks to Tavis Smiley, who first led me to believe that a book might be made out of the story of my life, and then went about making it so.

ABOUT THE AUTHOR

BETTY CHARBONNET REID SOSKIN is an author, composer and singer, social and political activist, entrepreneur, mother, grandmother, great-grandmother, historian, blogger, public speaker, and National Park Service ranger whose remarkable life spans the great American fault lines of the 20th and early 21st centuries.

Born into a Cajun/Creole African-American family, she spent her earliest years in New Orleans in the era of lynchings and Jim Crow segregation. Her family later settled in Oakland, California, following the historic floods that devastated the City of New Orleans in 1927. As a file clerk in an all-black segregated union hall during World War II, she was witness to the flood tide of black and white workers who poured into the Bay Area wartime shipyards, a mass migration that changed the face and social fabric of California and helped usher in the civil rights era.

Along with her first husband, Mel, Betty helped integrate the East Bay suburbs by moving their family into a previously white neighborhood. Betty and Mel also founded one of the first black-owned record shop businesses in California. After working with elected officials to rehabilitate the block on which the record shop was located, Betty served on the staff of a Berkeley City Council member and then as field representative to two members of the California State Assembly.

In the 1960s and '70s, she was active in the Bay Area's civil rights and Black Power movements, as well as the movement to end the Vietnam War.

In 1995 Betty was named a "Woman of the Year" by the California State Legislature. In 2005 she was named one of the nation's ten outstanding women, "Builders of communities and dreams," by the National Women's History Project in ceremonies in both Griffiths Park in Los Angeles and Washington, D.C.

As an Assembly field representative, Betty was instrumental in the establishment of Rosie the Riveter/World War II Home Front National Historical Park in Richmond, California, in 2000. She was later hired to work at the Rosie the Riveter Park as the oldest permanent park ranger in the National Park Service. She is a highly sought-after public speaker and her blog, *CBreaux Speaks*, has thousands of followers.

Betty continues to work for the National Park Service. She lives in Richmond, California.

ABOUT THE EDITOR

J. DOUGLAS ALLEN-TAYLOR is a novelist, editor, and award-winning journalist and columnist. He served full-time in the Black Freedom Movement for more than two decades in the 1960s, '70s, and '80s, most of them spent in the Deep South. He is the author of the historical novel *Sugaree Rising*, about the displacement of black landowners from a South Carolina community during the Depression. Allen-Taylor currently lives in his native Oakland, California.

CREDITS

Titles of Related Interest

BROTHER WEST: Living and Loving Out Loud, a Memoir,
by Cornel West

*PEACE FROM BROKEN PIECES: How to Get Through What You're
Going Through,* by Iyanla Vanzant

*PLAY LIFE MORE BEAUTIFULLY: Reflections on Music, Friendship &
Creativity, by Seymour Bernstein & Andrew Harvey*

All of the above are available at your local bookstore,
or may be ordered by contacting Hay House (see next page).

We hope you enjoyed this Hay House book. If you'd like to receive our online catalog featuring additional information on Hay House books and products, or if you'd like to find out more about the Hay Foundation, please contact:

Hay House, Inc., P.O. Box 5100, Carlsbad, CA 92018-5100
(760) 431-7695 or (800) 654-5126
(760) 431-6948 (fax) or (800) 650-5115 (fax)
www.hayhouse.com® • www.hayfoundation.org

———

Published and distributed in Australia by:
Hay House Australia Pty. Ltd., 18/36 Ralph St., Alexandria NSW 2015
Phone: 612-9669-4299 • *Fax:* 612-9669-4144 • www.hayhouse.com.au

Published and distributed in the United Kingdom by:
Hay House UK, Ltd., Astley House, 33 Notting Hill Gate, London W11 3JQ
Phone: 44-20-3675-2450 • *Fax:* 44-20-3675-2451 • www.hayhouse.co.uk

Published in India by: Hay House Publishers India,
Muskaan Complex, Plot No. 3, B-2, Vasant Kunj, New Delhi 110 070
Phone: 91-11-4176-1620 • *Fax:* 91-11-4176-1630 • www.hayhouse.co.in

Distributed in Canada by:
Raincoast Books, 2440 Viking Way, Richmond, B.C. V6V 1N2
Phone: 1-800-663-5714 • *Fax:* 1-800-565-3770 • www.raincoast.com

———

Access New Knowledge.
Anytime. Anywhere.

Learn and evolve at your own pace
with the world's leading experts.

www.hayhouseU.com